D1986753

John Green

Looking for Alaska

Teacher's Manual

by
Birgit Ohmsieder

Cornelsen

Contents

Introduction 3
Synopsis 3
Reading Journal 4
Pre-Reading Activities 5
Copymaster 1: Pre-Reading 7
Working With the Individual Chapters 8

before
Unit 1: Arriving at Culver Creek 13
Copymaster 2: Comprehension 15
Copymaster 3: Creating a Character Profile 16
Copymaster 4: The Labyrinth 17

Unit 2: Dr Hyde and the Smoking Hole 18
Copymaster 5: Read and Recap 20
Copymaster 6: Thinking about Teachers 21

Unit 3: A Comet Needs a Tail 22
Copymaster 7: Comprehension 24
Copymaster 8: Read, Reflect, Rewrite 25

Unit 4: Girlfriends 26
Copymaster 9: Life Questions 29
Copymaster 10: Feelings Mind Map 30
Copymaster 11: Working on Writing Tasks 31

Unit 5: Thanksgiving 32
Copymaster 12: Comprehension 34
Copymaster 13: Alaska's Hero 35

Unit 6: Pulling a Prank 36
Copymaster 14: The Narrator 38
Copymaster 15: Literary Terms 39

Unit 7: To Be Continued? 40
Copymaster 16: Reciprocal Reading 43
Copymaster 17: Cooperative Crossword (1) 44
Copymaster 18: Cooperative Crossword (2) 45
Copymaster 19: A Role-Play 46

after
Unit 8: Straight and Fast 47
Copymaster 20: Gap Summary 48
Copymaster 21: To Not Be Continued 49

Unit 9: Finding Out 50
Copymaster 22: Comprehension 53
Copymaster 23: Helping Miles 54

Unit 10: A Doodled Flower 55
Copymaster 24: Character Analysis 57

Unit 11: A Memorial Prank 58
Copymaster 25: Art and Empathy 59
Copymaster 26: Art Gallery Captions 60

Unit 12: Out of the Labyrinth 61
Copymaster 27: Let's Get It Right 63
Copymaster 28: Looking Back at the Novel 64

Post-Reading Activities 65
Ideas for Projects 67
Copymaster 29: Thinking Things Out 68

Written Tests 69
Copymaster 30: Written Test 1 71
Copymaster 31: Written Test 2 72

Teacher's Manual
John Green • **Looking for Alaska**

Erarbeitet von
Birgit Ohmsieder

Verlagsredaktion
Katrin Heinecke; Ralph Williams (Assistenz)

Technische Umsetzung
Eva Miller-Matthia, MatMil Translations and Desktop Publishing

Herausgeber der Cornelsen Senior English Library
Prof. Dr. Albert-Reiner Glaap

www.cornelsen.de

1. Auflage, 1. Druck 2011

© 2011 Cornelsen Verlag, Berlin

Das Werk und seine Teile sind urheberrechtlich geschützt. Jede Nutzung in anderen als den gesetzlich zugelassenen Fällen bedarf der vorherigen schriftlichen Einwilligung des Verlages. Hinweis zu §§ 46, 52 a UrhG: Weder das Werk noch seine Teile dürfen ohne eine solche Einwilligung eingescannt und in ein Netzwerk eingestellt oder sonst öffentlich zugänglich gemacht werden.
Dies gilt auch für Intranets von Schulen und sonstigen Bildungseinrichtungen.
Die Kopiervorlagen dürfen für den eigenen Unterrichtsgebrauch in der jeweils benötigten Anzahl vervielfältigt werden.

Druck: H. Heenemann, Berlin

ISBN 978-3-06-031126-2

Inhalt gedruckt auf säurefreiem Papier aus nachhaltiger Forstwirtschaft.

Introduction

Reasons for Teaching the Novel

Looking for Alaska has been hugely popular both in and beyond the USA, where it is now a set text in many high schools and colleges. Topics like love, sexuality, relationships, being an outsider and college life ensure the emotional identification of both male and female readers with the novel's characters. Larger issues like mortality, suicide, responsibility and grief also play a significant role and encourage deeper classroom discussion, thereby making the novel more profound than most teen fiction.

Narrated by a male teenager, *Looking for Alaska* has been criticized for its sexual content and its inclusion of characters that drink alcohol, smoke, take drugs and swear. However, to judge the book purely on its controversial content doesn't do it justice. Suggestions will be given for handling all of these topics in an adequate, meaningful and balanced manner. Teaching this novel is fun – the students' enthusiasm will rub off on you and vice versa!

General Remarks on the Suggested Teaching Approach

Looking for Alaska can be read in grade 10 or in a *Grundkurs*. If read step by step, the novel offers many opportunities for speculating and reflecting; teachers should therefore encourage students not to read ahead. The step-by-step approach also allows the teacher to give students language help if needed.

This manual trains basic skills relevant to the *Oberstufe* like creative writing and point of view or writing a summary, an essay, a letter or a characterization. It also offers a detailed synopsis of the novel (cf. p. 8ff.).

The manual suggests a variety of speaking, reading and writing activities which frequently make use of interactive learning modes. Pre-reading activities motivate, challenge and arouse the students' curiosity. If done carefully, the pre-reading tasks will prepare students well for the 'real' reading, allowing them to contribute their own experiences, ideas and speculations; individualization is one of the main teaching approaches of this manual. The teacher will select activities according to taste, amount of time available, group size and ability.

The novel has been divided into 12 teaching units. The manual offers one to four copymasters for each unit. There is always one comprehension activity which may be done before the suggested while-reading activities. At the end of each unit, the manual offers a pre-reading task for the next unit which prepares students for the upcoming topics. Teaching the novel will take about four weeks provided there are at least three lessons per week (i. e. one unit per lesson).

The post-reading activities encourage reflection of what has been read and enable the students to expand and enhance their own perception of the novel and the characters. Learning how to appreciate a literary work will increase the pleasure in further reading.

The section 'ideas for projects' offers ideas for student presentations or further reading on the novel, the author and topics related to the novel. The projects suggested go beyond the core understanding of the novel.

Two suggestions for written tests (*Klausuren*) offer different possibilities of testing the students' comprehension, analytical and critical skills: The teacher can choose either exam 1 with a sample extract from *Looking for Alaska* if he/she wants students to prove their understanding of the novel – or use exam 2 if students are to apply their insight into the novel to another text. The tests can be adapted to the needs of the various *Länder*.

The intention of the manual is to offer colleagues as much support as possible so that they can work successfully with the novel according to the students' needs. Whenever possible, solutions and alternatives are given for weaker or stronger groups (differentiation/*Differenzierung*).

Synopsis

'Tonight, we were invincible', Miles Halter thinks when he feels close to 'the Great Perhaps' he set out to seek when leaving his Florida home to go to boarding school in Alabama. Miles, the nerdy outsider who is good at remembering people's last words, meets friends there who accept him the way he is. There is Chip, his loyal roommate and Alaska, the mysterious, green-eyed and beautiful girl Miles immediately falls in love with. Together with Takumi, a boy of Japanese descent and Lara from Romania, the five of them live through the ups and downs of college life, playing pranks on the Weekday Warriors, children of wealthy families who return home every weekend. Miles is fascinated by Alaska who likes reading poems and novels and who wants to find the way out of life's labyrinth of suffering. One night Alaska leaves campus abruptly and dies in a car accident. Miles and Chip feel guilty because they didn't keep her from leaving although she was terribly drunk. The two of them set out to discover the truth about Alaska's death. Miles is heartbroken because he loved her and will never find out whether she loved him back. After weeks of trying to discover whether Alaska committed suicide or not, Miles and Chip give up. In the end, Miles realizes that the only way out of life's labyrinth is forgiveness. He is finally able to forgive both Alaska for leaving him and himself for letting her go.

Birgit Ohmsieder

Reading Journal

Students should be made aware that noting down any ideas, thoughts, questions and comments they have during the reading process will help them reflect on their reading and help them gain better insights.

Here are some suggestions on how to keep a reading journal.

Note: Each student's reading journal will be different and they need not all follow the same structure.

An overview

While reading, students should be encouraged to keep track of events by taking notes. This chapter-by-chapter or unit-by-unit overview (see p. 8 for an example) will help them to

– get an overview of the novel;
– easily locate scenes or quotes when working on tasks;
– formulate a summary.

There are different ways of keeping an overview.

Example 1

Unit/Chapter (page)	What happens	Comments/ Questions	Vocabulary (page/line)

'Comments/Questions': Phrasing questions can help students understand what they are reading. Similarly, answering questions may help to understand the plot, the structure of the novel, the characters and their problems. Here are some examples of questions students may want to answer:

– Why is the narrator telling this story?
– Does this remind you of other novels you have read or of your own life experiences? Is it relevant to your life?
– How might the story continue?

'Vocabulary': In addition to including important new vocabulary items in the overview, it may also be a good idea to start a separate vocabulary log. Teachers should point out that vocabulary logs are individualized. They include unfamiliar words which each student likes or considers important and which he or she would like to use actively. Vocabulary can either be kept as a list or in a table. Example:

Word	Example	Collocation	Definition
minor (adj, n) (p. 7, l. 2)	a) 'my minor life' b) 'serve alcohol to minors'	a minor detail	a) not very important b) a teen-ager / young person (not an adult)

Note: Students should

– not choose more than five or six new words for every few chapters;
– practise using the words in class as well as in their homework.

Example 2

Unit/ Chapter	Who?	What?	When?	Where?	Why? (Comments)

Summaries

While summaries may give an overview of a novel's structure, it is not necessary for each student to write a coherent summary of every chapter or unit. Summaries may also be made in note form or students can pool their results, each one furnishing classmates with his or her chapter or unit summary and receiving summaries from classmates in return.

If chapters or units are of similar length, one possible method of doing this is the jigsaw puzzle (see p. 36, unit 6, notes on copymaster 14).

Character profile

Profiles of the different characters can also become part of the reading journal (see copymaster 3, p. 16). In addition, students can also answer the following questions:

– What do you like about the characters? What don't you like?
– What do you think of how they act in the novel?

Creative writing

Any relevant creative writing tasks should be included in the reading journal. These may include

– writing a diary entry for one of the characters;
– interviewing one of the characters;
– writing a newspaper article about an event in the novel;
– retelling a passage from another character's point of view;
– adding a passage to explain events not explained in the novel.

For further suggestions, see Post-Reading Activities, p. 65.

Suggested reading chunks

The novel is divided into twelve units which serve as suggested reading chunks. Where it is advisable to read only part of a unit and do a certain task before continuing the novel, this is marked in the teacher's notes.

Pre-Reading Activities

Pre-Reading ➢ Copymaster 1

NOTES

Copymaster 1 prepares students for the upcoming topics and allows them to speculate based on quotes from the book. This approach also demands that students actively look out for the context of these quotes as they read.

1 Brainstorming

Students work in groups of four. They exchange their ideas and present them to the class. The teacher can also bring pictures related to the topics and have students brainstorm on that basis.
If students' results are too general, the teacher may give them the following for more specific results: Why do people read books? Think of as many reasons as you can. What words do you associate with love? Brainstorm them. What do you imagine college life to be like? Write a list of adjectives. Where have you seen or read about labyrinths before?
Alternative: Each group deals with one topic. Students then form new groups of four with one student from each of the former groups and exchange their ideas.

2 Mental video

The aim of the task is to be as precise as possible linguistically. The teacher may read out one of the following passages to the students:
a p. 109 ll. 23–30 (from 'before'): 'Then we turned north, [...] walk back to the barn, triumphant.'
b p. 141 ll. 15–21 (from 'after'): 'For a moment, [...] shocked out of air.'
Example for **b**:
see: blank faces of students in (a state of) shock
hear: nothing; absolute/dead silence
feel: devastated; despair, shock

3 Typically male, typically female?

Words to be dictated: books, prank, lake, smoke, death, life, curves, skinny, muscles, coffee table, wine, drunk, bad conscience, white flowers, accident
Students should be able to explain their choice.

4 Life questions

Students may decide on their own whether they want to work alone, in pairs or in groups. All questions are collected and grouped (if possible). Most questions will remain unanswered, yet may show that most adolescents, like Miles and Alaska, are often troubled by profound philosophical questions no one can really give them an answer for.

NB: This task should not be done if the teacher decides to do the essay-writing task in unit 4, copymaster 9, task 4.

5 Speculating

Collect students' speculations and present them in the classroom (wall newspaper). At the end of unit 1, students compare their speculations with the actual events.

6 Now you

Answers may include whether or not students think the pranks were fun and whether or not they were punished. Because some of the answers may be very personal and some may not want to share their experience with the whole class, students should not be forced to present their results in class.

ADDITIONAL TASK

Alaska and Miles are both atypical representatives of their sex, whereas Chip and Sara are the stereotypical male and female. If teachers wish to work on sexual stereotyping, students can do the following task:
Imagine the following situation: you have met a boy/girl at a party. You think he/she is totally cute and you want to see him/her again. What do you do? Make a plan. Then exchange your ideas with a partner or in a group.

Collect the answers on the board and analyse them: are there plans of action more common for one sex? Students make notes and form either mixed groups or groups of boys and girls only. In groups of girls or boys only, students may brainstorm in a 'safe' environment. In mixed groups, the opposite sex can give feedback on possible approaches. If they wish, each group may then present their results to the class.

Looking at the Outside – The Cover

Note: After students have chosen and worked on three or four of the pre-reading tasks on copymaster 1, they may also discuss the following ('Looking at the Outside' and 'Looking at the Inside') together in class.

Invite students to speculate (in small groups or with a partner) on the implications of the title page: first just the words, then taking into consideration the title page's various illustrated elements (blown-out candle, white tulips and female face). After any initial speculations concerning the title page, the blurb on the back cover should help to correctly interpret the name 'Alaska'. Students may then come to different conclusions on what exactly 'looking for' might mean in the context of the novel.

Looking at the Inside – Leafing Through the Book

Invite students to leaf through the book and comment on what strikes them. They may speculate on why they think things were done as they were. They may notice

- the division of the novel into two parts, 'before' and 'after' as well as the fact that there are as many days 'before' as there are 'after' (136), although the first part is significantly longer than the second;
- different chapter lengths, chapter titles merely as a countdown, no table of contents or numbered chapters, layout, typeface.

This is a good opportunity for students to revise their vocabulary for describing books (as opposed to talking about novels).

Opening Lines

Invite students to read the opening lines of the novel (ll. 1–13) and describe the situation:

1 What is the importance of a going-away party in a teenager's life? List some of the things the protagonist seems to expect of the students at his new school (by contrast with those at his old one).

2 Comment on the effect of the opening lines: do they make you want to read on? Give reasons.

3 Comment on the opening lines as the reader's introduction to the protagonist. Is it a good 'first impression'?

4 What idea do you get of the protagonist's life? What expectations does this create for the rest of the novel?

Ask students to number the chapters for easier reference and orientation, e.g. when working on their reading journal.

Pre-Reading

NOTE

Choose three or four of the following tasks and work with classmates who chose the same tasks.

TASKS

1 Brainstorming

What do you associate with the topics love/sex, college life, books, labyrinth? Brainstorm anything that comes to mind. Then agree on the five most relevant expressions or words for each topic.

2 Mental video

Close your eyes and listen to a short extract from the novel.

THINK: Visualize what happens.

PAIR: Tell a partner what you saw, heard and felt.

SHARE: Exchange your impressions with another pair.

3 Typically male, typically female?

Make two columns, one for 'male' and one for 'female'. Your teacher will dictate a list of words.

THINK: In which of the two columns does the word fit best? Do not think about your decision for too long; act on impulse.

PAIR: Compare your list with your partner.

SHARE: Discuss your results with another pair.

4 Life questions

Collect questions you have about life in general. Decide on the most important question and describe how you would look for an answer to it.

5 Speculating

Read the quotes below taken from the first three chapters of the novel. Speculate and make notes on

- **a** what will happen in the novel;
- **b** where the action is set;
- **c** who the main characters are and what their problems are;
- **d** the main theme(s) of the novel.

To say that I had low expectations would be to underestimate the matter dramatically.

The only thing worse than having a party that no one attended is having a party attended only by two vastly, deeply uninteresting people.

I ought to cry, but I'd lived with my parents for sixteen years, and a trial separation seemed overdue.

Things never happened like I imagined them.

I stared, stunned partly by the force of the voice emanating from the petite (but God, curvy) girl and partly by the gigantic stacks of books that lined her walls.

'So what's the labyrinth?' I asked her.
'You figure out what the labyrinth is and how to get out of it, and I'll get you laid.'

'Is the labyrinth living or dying? Which is he trying to escape – the world or the end of it?'

'There are people with real problems. I've got real problems.'

I went to bed wearing a T-shirt […] feeling – probably for the first time in my life – the fear and excitement of living in a place where you never know what's going to happen or when.

6 Now you

Discuss the following questions with a partner or in a group. If you like, share your answers in class.

- **a** Have you ever played or experienced a prank at school? Describe what happened.
- **b** Name five characteristics a good friend should have. Be prepared to explain why you think so.

© 2011 Cornelsen Verlag, Berlin. Alle Rechte vorbehalten.

Working With the Individual Chapters

Overview

before

No./Page	Chapter	Content
Unit 1	**Arriving at Culver Creek**	
1 7–9	one hundred thirty-six days before	Miles Halter leaves his Florida home for an Alabama boarding school. Two classmates turn up for his farewell party.
2 10–25	one hundred twenty-eight days before	At Culver Creek, Miles meets his roommate Chip (nicknamed 'the Colonel') and Alaska Young, a rebellious girl Miles is instantly attracted to. Miles is nicknamed 'Pudge' for being so skinny.
3 25–33	one hundred twenty-seven days before	Miles meets the school's dean Mr Starnes (nicknamed 'the Eagle') and Takumi, who watches him eat his first bufriedos. During one of his first nights, three students take Miles from his bed, tape his arms to his body and his legs together and throw him into a nearby lake. Chip is shocked and promises to take revenge.
Unit 2	**Dr Hyde and the Smoking Hole**	
4 33–38	one hundred twenty-six days before	The next morning Chip notices that the boys who abducted Miles also urinated into his shoes. He is furious. Miles has his first French class and realizes that he will have to work hard at Culver Creek. He also meets Dr Hyde, an elderly, rather frail teacher he likes immediately.
5 38–42	one hundred twenty-two days before	Miles finds Chip in their room trying to iron a shirt for a date with his girlfriend Sara. When Sara comes to pick Chip up they have an argument and Sara leaves. Later that evening Chip finds out that Sara thinks he reported Marya and Paul, two students who were expelled a year earlier.
6 42–48	one hundred ten days before	One day Miles is thrown out of Dr Hyde's class for being inattentive. Alaska protests and is also told to leave. Miles is upset because he is so fond of this teacher. After class, Miles, Chip, Alaska and Takumi leave the college grounds to walk to a place in the woods close to the creek which they call the 'Smoking Hole'. They discuss who reported Marya and Paul.
Unit 3	**A Comet Needs a Tail**	
7 48–54	one hundred nine days before	Chip takes Miles to the first basketball game of the season. Although Miles hates everything to do with sports, he still accompanies Chip. During the game Kevin (who played the prank on Miles) approaches them and offers a truce. Miles and Chip don't want a truce and make a bet which Kevin loses. Because the Culver Creek team is rather weak, Chip shouts abuse at the opposing team until the referee tells him to leave the gym. Miles follows him.
8 54	one hundred eight days before	Dr Hyde talks to Miles one day after class. He advises him to take the Buddhist belief of being truly present every minute of one's life more seriously.
9 54–56	one hundred one days before	Alaska takes a couple of students to McDonald's in her car to give them a lesson in precalculus because exams are soon. On the way there, a girl called Lara sits on Miles's lap.
10 56–59	one hundred days before	One day Alaska tells Miles why she is called Alaska and what her name means. Miles wants to kiss her.
11 59–60	ninety-nine days before	Mr Starnes catches Miles, Chip, Takumi and Alaska by the lake. Since Chip and Alaska were smoking, he orders the four of them to come to the Jury the next day to receive their punishment.
12 60–63	ninety-eight days before	Told not to say anything in front of the Jury, Miles doesn't. Chip and Alaska are given ten hours of doing dishes, whereas Takumi and Miles are not punished. Miles is admonished by Mr Starnes not to abuse his privileges.

No./Page	Chapter	Content
Unit 4	**Girlfriends**	
13 63–65	eighty-nine days before	Alaska tells Miles that she has found a girlfriend for him and planned a triple date for the upcoming weekend with her and her boyfriend Jake, Chip and Sara, and Miles and Lara.
14 65–70	eighty-seven days before	On the weekend Miles meets Jake for the first time. The seven of them go to watch another basketball game at the gym. As usual Chip provokes the opposing team. As a result Miles is hit hard by a ball. He has a concussion, vomits on Lara's jeans and is taken to hospital. Back at college, Chip tells Miles that Sara has broken up with him.
15 71–72	eighty-four days before	It rains for days. Miles notices that Alaska only makes rare appearances. When trying to talk to her she indicates that she does not want to be asked any questions.
16 73–75	seventy-six days before	Dr Hyde gives the students the question for their final exam. Alaska is angry because some students flooded her room and many of her books are now seriously damaged. Chip promises to punish those responsible.
17 75–78	sixty-seven days before	One day Takumi asks Miles to join him for a walk, where he tells Miles that Alaska was the one who reported ('ratted on') Marya and Paul. Miles is shocked, but now understands why Alaska and Chip took the blame in front of the Jury.
18 78–83	fifty-eight days before	Alaska wakes Miles up early on a Saturday morning to persuade him to stay at Culver Creek with her over Thanksgiving. Miles calls his parents and lies to them, saying that he has exams to study for. His mother is disappointed and Miles has a bad conscience. Chip warns him not to start a relationship with Alaska, saying it would mean trouble.
Unit 5	**Thanksgiving**	
19 84–86	fifty-two days before	After everyone has left, Alaska and Miles are alone on campus. Alaska shows Miles where she hides her wine. They spend the evening outside together. Alaska reads from Kurt Vonnegut's *Cat's Cradle* and puts her hand on Miles's leg. Miles is about to tell Alaska that he loves her when she interrupts him, saying that to her the labyrinth is all about suffering.
20 86–89	fifty-one days before	The next morning Alaska wakes Miles up. They enter Kevin's room, where they find a lot of haircare products. They leave the room through the window and go to the Smoking Hole.
21 89–92	forty-nine days before	Alaska invites Miles to go and search the other rooms for porn movies. They find all sorts of things and Miles realizes that Alaska must have done this before. Finally they find a porn movie and watch it together. Alaska falls asleep on the couch and Miles is desperate to be close to her. He is fond of Alaska, but she seems out of his reach.
22 92–96	forty-seven days before	Alaska and Miles build a huge candle out of dripping wax in Alaska's room. Chip arrives at lunchtime and invites them home for Thanksgiving. They meet his mother, Dolores, who lives in a trailer park. Chip is ashamed of his poor home, but Dolores is an excellent cook.
23 96–97	forty-six days before	On Thanksgiving Day everyone is in a good mood. They cherish the food and wine and list what they are thankful for.
24 97–99	forty-four days before	Back at college, Alaska takes Miles to the liquor store where she always buys her wine and cigarettes with her fake ID. She tells him about jokes her mother told her when she was little. The same day she comes to see Miles in his room crying. She tells him that she messes things up and that she is upset. Although he finds it hard to cope with Alaska's changing moods and does not really know what she is talking about, Miles still tries to console her.
Unit 6	**Pulling a Prank**	
25 99–101	christmas	All students go home for Christmas. Miles studies a lot for his exams and enjoys being with his parents.
26 101–103	eight days before	After the Christmas break Alaska suggests they play a prank to take revenge on Kevin and his friends. Miles is annoyed about the fact that he is left out when Chip and Alaska set out to plan the prank.
27 103–104	four days before	While Chip and Alaska are planning the prank, Miles prepares for his exams and even manages to finish his religion essay.

No./Page	Chapter	Content
28 104–114	three days before	After the exams Miles, Takumi, Lara, Chip and Alaska set out to play the prank. All of them pretend to spend the weekend somewhere else for different reasons and leave the campus. They all meet at the barn and Chip reads out his plan. Miles and Takumi are to light firecrackers to lure Mr Starnes out of his house. At the same time, Lara is going to put blue dye in some boys' haircare products, while Chip and Alaska are going to use Mr Starnes' computer to send out reports to some parents saying that their children have failed classes. Almost everything goes well and they meet back at the barn and sleep there.
Unit 7	**To Be Continued?**	
29 114–126	two days before	The next morning they have a freestyle rap contest. In the afternoon Alaska decides it's time to get drunk. She asks everybody to tell the others about the best and the worst days in their lives. Only the winner of each round does not have to drink. They learn that Alaska's mother died of an aneurysm when she was eight years old. In the end they are all quite drunk and Miles kisses Lara, with whom he shares a sleeping bag.
30 126–127	one day before	Early the next morning Chip wakes the others up. They are all hung-over and walk back to the campus. They check in with Mr Starnes, go back to their rooms and sleep.
31 127–135	the last day	The next morning Kevin enters Miles and Chip's room. His hair is blue and he offers a truce which Chip refuses. Miles spends the afternoon with Lara who offers to perform oral sex on him. Since both of them do not really know how to do it, they ask Alaska for help. They try again and Miles has his first orgasm with a girl. Miles spends the evening with Chip and Alaska. Alaska flirts with Miles and seduces him, they kiss and both fall asleep. The phone rings. When she returns from the phone, Alaska insists she has to leave. Miles and Chip help distract Mr Starnes and Alaska drives off although she is drunk.

after

Unit 8	**Straight and Fast**	
32 139–145	the day after	The next morning Mr Starnes wakes up all the students and asks them to come to the gym. Miles notices that Alaska is not among the crowd. In tears, Mr Starnes tells them that Alaska was killed in an accident the night before. Everyone is shocked and Miles feels guilty. Incredulous, he assumes that this might be another trick Alaska is playing on them until Mr Starnes tells him that he saw Alaska and that she had hit a police car. Walking back to his room, Miles is aware of the fact that he will never know what Alaska's last words were.
33 145–149	two days after	Miles can't sleep all night and is tormented by feelings of loss. Chip tries to distract himself by learning things by heart. All of a sudden he leaves the room with his almanac. Miles wonders whether he had mattered to Alaska at all and whether she had wanted to go and see Jake that night. Lara comes to talk to him but he doesn't want to talk to her. He has a nightmare and is all alone because Chip hasn't returned.
34 149–151	four days after	Two days later Chip returns at 5 a.m., freezing because he has walked 82 miles without a break. He tells Miles that he had been fed up with Alaska's moods.
35 151–153	six days after	On Sunday all students attend Alaska's funeral. Takumi, Lara, Chip and Miles go by car, avoiding the spot where Alaska died. On the way to the funeral Miles is in tears at the idea that Alaska might have loved him back. Though he had hoped to see her again he finds the casket closed. Alaska's father tells him that she had wanted it to be that way. Chip and Miles stand close to the casket and Miles tells Alaska that he loves her.
36 153–157	seven days after	Miles finds himself incapable of doing anything because he feels guilty about Alaska's death. In her room, Miles is overwhelmed by the smell of her which lingers in her belongings. Together with Chip he looks through her books and finds *The General in his Labyrinth*. He finds a passage that had been underlined by Alaska and the words 'straight and fast' scribbled in the margin. Chip and Miles think that those words might explain why she drove into the police car.
37 158–160	eight days after	In class the teachers talk to the students and ask them how they feel. Dr Hyde reads out Alaska's question for her final essay. Miles thinks that everybody has a better excuse to grieve for Alaska than Chip and himself, since the others didn't kill her.

No./Page	Chapter	Content
Unit 9	**Finding Out**	
38 160–162	nine days after	The next day Chip tells Miles that it might have been Jake who called that night and that Alaska had wanted to go and see him and then killed herself. Miles is furious because finding out who called won't bring Alaska back. Chip sympathizes but tells Miles that he has made a plan to help them find out what happened that night. Although he doesn't really want to find out, Miles gives in because he doesn't want to lose Chip as a friend.
39 162–166	thirteen days after	A few days later, Chip and Miles walk to the police station to talk to the officer who witnessed the accident. He cannot tell them whether it was an accident or not. But he tells them how high her blood alcohol level was and that he saw tulips on the backseat. On the way back, Miles repeats that he doesn't want to find out why Alaska died. He thinks Chip is unable to understand him. Chip convinces him that it is important for them to stay friends, so Miles agrees to help him find out more.
40 166–169	fourteen days after	The next day Miles and Chip do some research on the reasons people commit suicide. They can't draw any clear conclusions from what they find on the Internet, they only know that the phone call must have influenced Alaska's decision to kill herself. Though they don't gain any new insights Chip insists that they carry on. Another student comes to see them to tell them that she thinks Alaska has sent her a sign, which both Chip and Miles consider to be a rather stupid idea.
41 169–173	twenty days after	When Chip tells Miles that he wants to call Jake to find out what happened the night Alaska died, they start arguing. Angry at Chip for asking why he didn't keep Alaska from leaving that night, Miles goes to the Smoking Hole. Sitting there he remembers Alaska and everything she taught him. He is upset because he understands that she was the one who helped him change into the person he has become. He walks back to the dorm where the boys apologize to each other. Chip tells him that he has changed his mind and that he has postponed calling Jake.
42 173–175	twenty-one days after	Dr Hyde tells the students about Karl Marx's famous quote that 'religion is the opiate of the masses', which makes Miles consider the possibility of an afterlife and reflect on where Alaska might be now. After class he goes to McDonald's with Takumi where they admit to one another how much they miss Alaska.
43 175–182	twenty-seven days after	Chip wants to get drunk to find out how drunk Alaska was when she hit the police car. To be able to do so, Chip and Miles steal Mr Starnes's Breathalyzer. Takumi is annoyed that he is not allowed to take part in this plan. The two boys stay up in their room where Chip drinks as much as he can while Miles uses the Breathalyzer to measure the amount of alcohol in his blood. In the middle of their experiment, Mr Starnes knocks on their door. They manage to fool him, but Miles has to appear before the Jury for smoking in his room. They come to the conclusion that Alaska was definitely too drunk to drive.
44 182–183	twenty-eight days after	Because of their investigations, Miles has neglected his studies, but he doesn't really care. Chip decides they have to call Jake as he is the only one who might help them find out more. They finally let Takumi in on what happened the night Alaska left.
Unit 10	**A Doodled Flower**	
45 184–188	twenty-nine days after	The following day Chip finally calls Jake to find out what Alaska told him the night she left. While Chip is on the phone, Miles and Takumi argue because Takumi is tired of Miles thinking he was the only boy Alaska cared about. Chip reports what Jake told him on the phone. They know that the phone call must have played a crucial role, but Jake can't provide them with any clues on why Alaska left so suddenly.
46 188–189	thirty-seven days after	The following week Miles meets Lara by chance. She looks at him angrily, but they don't talk. Miles feels awful for not talking to Lara, but the only thing he cares about is finding out why and how Alaska died.

No./Page	Chapter	Content
47 189–191	forty-five days after	Takumi, Miles and Chip go to the liquor store to buy cigarettes. Once more they all notice how much they miss Alaska.
48 191–194	forty-six days after	Takumi convinces Miles to finally talk to Lara. He goes to her room and apologizes for having ignored her for so long. They go for a walk and talk about Alaska. In the evening Chip, Miles, Lara and Takumi go to the Smoking Hole and throw cigarettes into the water in memory of Alaska. Again they try to figure out whether Alaska's death was an accident or suicide. Since their investigations have come to a dead end, Chip decides to give up.
49 194–196	fifty-one days after	Miles takes up studying for his classes again. In Religion he learns that everything that comes together falls apart and Miles thinks a lot about the sentence. Whereas Chip has given up on finding out why Alaska died, Miles still hopes to find the answer.
50 196–198	sixty-two days after	While calling his parents the following Sunday from the college payphone, Miles studies the notes scribbled on the wall. He discovers a flower which Alaska must have drawn while she was talking to Jake. He shows it to Chip. Both conclude that a sudden thought she had while drawing the flower must have led to her sudden departure.
Unit 11	**A Memorial Prank**	
51 198–199	sixty-nine days after	Miles is frustrated because it seems he will never find the reason for Alaska's death. He and Chip decide that they should plan a prank in memory of Alaska.
52 199–200	eighty-three days after	Chip plans the memorial prank and presents it to Miles, Takumi and Lara.
53 200–202	eighty-four days after	Miles calls his father because he needs his help to carry out the prank. His father agrees to fool Mr Starnes by pretending to be Dr Morse, a university professor from Florida doing research on adolescent sexuality. Mr Starnes is fooled.
54 202–209	one hundred two days after	They invite a professional stripper who is going to pretend to be the professor from Florida making a speech at Culver Creek's annual Speaker Day. The whole junior class knows about the prank, but nobody tells Mr Starnes. On Speaker Day the fake Dr Morse comes, steps up on the stage, reads out the speech Chip and Miles prepared for him and then starts stripping. After the event Mr Starnes orders Miles, Chip, Lara and Takumi to never do it again, but he takes the event in good humour.
Unit 12	**Out of the Labyrinth**	
55 209–210	one hundred fourteen days after	A week after the prank, Takumi provides Chip and Miles with the final clue about Alaska's death. He tells them that the day she left campus was January 10, the anniversary of her mother's death. They deduce that the flower she doodled on the wall while talking to Jake reminded her of the anniversary and assume she had a bad conscience for forgetting it.
56 210–213	one hundred eighteen days after	Though they still don't know whether Alaska's death was suicide or an accident, they finally give up on wanting to find out. Miles and Chip decide to drive through the spot on the highway where the accident happened.
57 213	one hundred nineteen days after	Miles, Chip, Lara and Takumi study laboriously for their finals and Miles misses Alaska because Chip is not as good a Maths teacher as she was.
58 213–215	one hundred twenty-two days after	In Religion, Dr Hyde gives the students the task for their annual final paper. He asks them to discuss Alaska's central question, how to get out of 'this labyrinth of suffering'.
59 215–219	one hundred thirty-six days after	One day before his parents come to pick him up, Miles finds a letter from Takumi, telling him and Chip that he was mad at them because they did not include him in their investigations about Alaska's death. He reveals that he met Alaska just before she got into her car the night she died. She had been looking for flowers to put on her mother's grave. Having read Takumi's letter, Miles understands that one crucial aspect of coping with life is forgiveness. With this insight, he is able to write his final essay in one go. He is at peace with himself knowing that he will never know whether her death was an accident or suicide, but he understands that he doesn't have to feel guilty about it any longer.

Preliminary Note

Several characters in the novel are given nicknames: Miles = 'Pudge', Chip = 'the Colonel', Mr Starnes = 'the Eagle', Dr Hyde = 'the Old Man'. In this manual, they will be referred to by their real names.

Unit 1: Arriving at Culver Creek

Summary – 'before'

The first chapter (pp. 7–9) introduces us to Miles Halter, his parents and two of his classmates who attend his farewell party. Quoting Rabelais, Miles explains that he doesn't want to wait until he dies to 'seek a Great Perhaps'.

The second chapter (pp. 10–25) describes Miles's arrival at Culver Creek Preparatory School and his introduction to his roommate Chip Martin as well as Alaska Young, who Miles is fascinated by. While Chip shows Miles the Smoking Hole and gives him advice to never report anyone, Alaska talks to him about books. She quotes Simón Bolívar's last words from one of her favourites, *The General in His Labyrinth*: 'How will I ever get out of this labyrinth!' Alaska promises to find Miles a girlfriend if he finds out what the labyrinth is and how to get out of it.

The third chapter (pp. 25–33) picks up the topic of reporting others. The discussion at the school cafeteria revolves around Marya and Paul, two students who were expelled the year before, presumably because someone reported them. That night an initiation prank is played on Miles: with his arms taped to his body, his legs taped together and his mouth covered with tape, he is thrown into the lake. Miles manages to swim back to the shore and free himself. When he tells Chip what happened, his roommate is outraged at the seriousness of the prank – Miles could have died – and promises to take revenge.

Unit 1 ➢ Copymaster 2

ANSWERS

1 1b; 2d; 3e; 4a; 5c
2 1c; 2e; 3a; 4b; 5d
3 1d; 2a; 3f; 4b; 5c; 6e

Unit 1 ➢ Copymaster 3

NOTES

After reading the first three chapters and before working on the tasks for unit 1, students compare their speculations (pre-reading) with what actually happened.

1 Keeping a character profile
The character profile can be done in pair- or group work. The teacher can also divide the class into three groups, each group working on a different character. Students then form new groups and exchange their information. Creating a character profile should be an ongoing reading assignment.

POSSIBLE ANSWERS

1 Keeping a character profile

	Miles	Chip	Alaska
outward appearance	skinny, lanky, 'chicken legs'	short, muscular, well-built, brown hair	good-looking, green eyes, 'curvy'
family background	middle-class family, caring parents, slightly overprotective mother, father also went to Culver Creek	scholarship holder, poor family, parents do not live together, father: truck driver and alcoholic	scholarship holder, from Vine Station, a small and depressing town in Alabama, her boyfriend Jake studies at Vanderbilt University (Tennessee)
likes/dislikes	likes reading, knows the last words of famous people, would like a girlfriend	knows all the countries of the world, sporty, likes Maths	likes reading, owns a lot of books she buys second-hand, *The General in His Labyrinth* is one of her favourites, smokes a lot
character traits	rather self-conscious, shy, quiet, not very popular at his old school, helpful	helpful, loyal, self-confident	moody, flirtatious, self-confident, rambunctious

2 Justifying your opinion
Individual answers.

Unit 1 ➢ Copymaster 4

NOTES

1 Students should make a note in their reading journals whenever the labyrinth is mentioned.

1c

Yoan Capote
Born in Cuba in 1977, Capote lives and works in Havana. He studied painting, but prefers sculpture. He won the UNESCO prize for his work in 2000.

'Open Mind'
The sculpture is a model of the human brain which looks like a maze in which Capote hopes to inspire us to reflect on how we interact within an urban environment. It is one of his most famous works.

2

Gabriel García Márquez
García Márquez (born 1927) is a Colombian novelist, screenwriter and journalist. He was awarded the Nobel Prize in 1982 and is considered one of the most important authors of the 20th century.

The General in His Labyrinth
The historical novel about Simón Bolívar, a Colombian leader and liberator, was published in 1989. It is a fictionalized account of Bolívar's attempt to leave South America for exile in Europe. The novel explores the labyrinth of Bolívar's life through the narrative of his memories.

3 The teacher collects the letters and redistributes them so that everyone has someone else's letter which they then answer from the point of view of Mr or Mrs Halter.

POSSIBLE ANSWERS

1a lose your orientation; only one way out; a challenge; maze/amazing; built for the man-eating Minotaur by Dedalus

1b Questions asked: 'What's the labyrinth?' (Miles); 'Is the labyrinth living or dying? Which is he trying to escape – the world or the end of it?' (Alaska)

1c The sculpture shows people walking around in a brain that is cut open and exposed. A stair leads into each cerebral hemisphere; it is possible to enter the brain's left hemisphere, walk through it as through a maze or labyrinth, and exit it through the right hemisphere.

1d–3 Individual answers.

Unit 1 – Comprehension

NOTE

Read pp. 7–33. Then put the sentences below into the correct order.

TASKS

1 one hundred thirty-six days before

- **a** He does not want to wait until he dies to seek 'a Great Perhaps'.
- **b** Miles Halter is about to leave his Florida home for an Alabama boarding school.
- **c** The evening ends with Miles and his parents watching TV together.
- **d** Miles is not particularly disappointed when only two of his classmates turn up at the farewell party his mother organized for him.
- **e** After the guests have left, his parents ask him why he wants to go to boarding school.

2 one hundred twenty-eight days before

- **a** Chip then introduces him to Alaska Young who fascinates Miles both by her looks and by the amount of books in her room.
- **b** They talk about books and Alaska tells Miles that *The General in his Labyrinth* is one of her favourites.
- **c** Miles unpacks and inspects the room he is going to share with a student called Chip Martin, who arrives shortly after him.
- **d** She promises to find him a girlfriend if he finds out what the labyrinth is and how to get out of it.
- **e** Chip tells Miles that he should never give away students who break the college rules.

3 one hundred twenty-seven days before

- **a** They talk about two students who were expelled for various offences the year before.
- **b** Miles manages to swim back to the shore and free himself from the tape around his body.
- **c** He walks back to the dorm and tells Chip what happened.
- **d** Chip takes Miles to the school cafeteria where he meets Takumi and eats bufriedos for the first time.
- **e** Chip is shocked and promises to take revenge.
- **f** At night three students take Miles from his bed, tape his arms to his body and his legs together and throw him into a nearby lake.

© 2011 Cornelsen Verlag, Berlin. Alle Rechte vorbehalten.

Unit 1 – Creating a Character Profile

TASKS

1 Keeping a character profile

While reading pp. 7–33, take notes on the following characters and fill in the table below. Complete their character profile as you read the novel. You can also add categories of your own, e.g. favourite last words.

	Miles	**Chip**	**Alaska**
outward appearance			
family background			
likes/ dislikes			
character traits			

2 Justifying your opinion

Who of the three adolescents do you like best? Give reasons. Explain whether or not you would like to have him/her as a friend.

© 2011 Cornelsen Verlag, Berlin. Alle Rechte vorbehalten.

Unit 1 – The Labyrinth

TASKS

1 Beyond the text

a With a partner, brainstorm ideas for the 'labyrinth'.

b Re-read what Alaska says about the labyrinth (p. 22, l. 22 – p. 23, l. 29 and p. 24, ll. 30–31). Which questions are asked in their conversation? Add questions of your own.

c Describe the sculpture below made by the Cuban sculptor Yoan Capote in 2008. Then brainstorm ideas for a title.

d With your partner, discuss whether Alaska would have liked the sculpture. Explain.

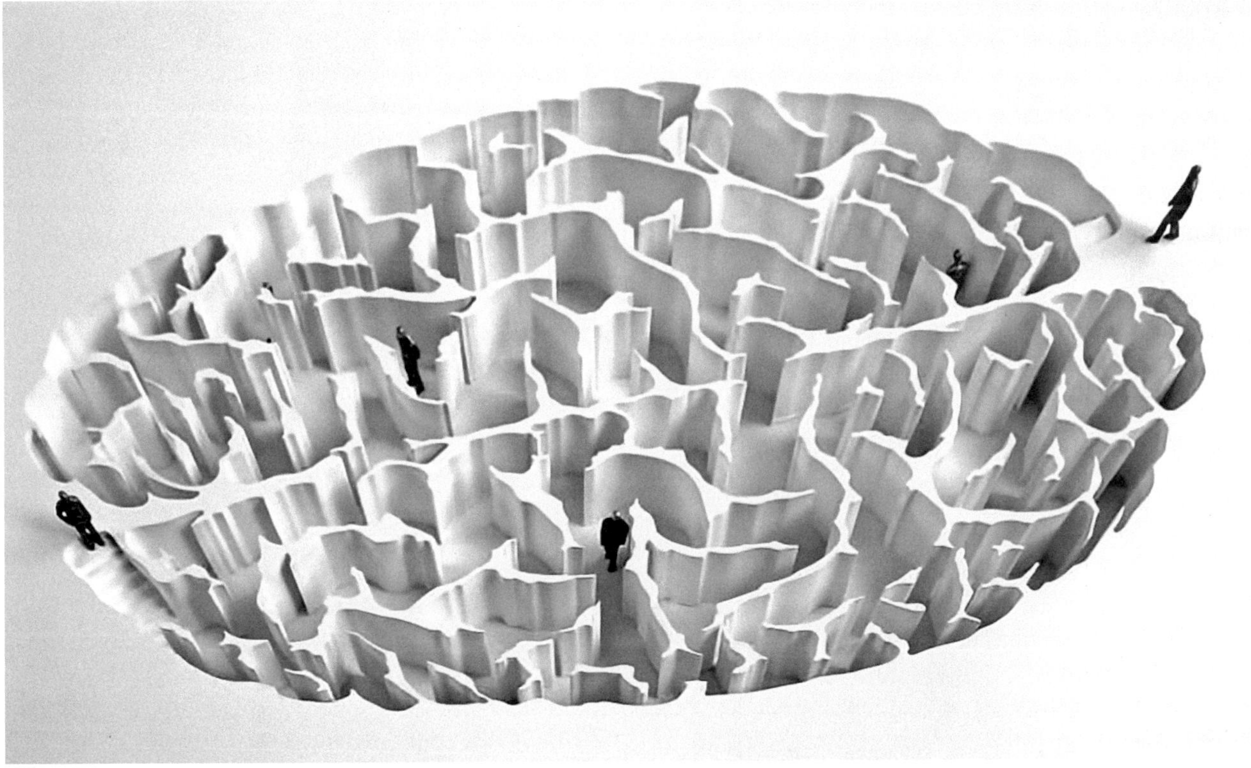

2 Doing research

In groups of four, research Gabriel García Márquez and *The General in His Labyrinth* and pool your results. Discuss whether it helps you answer the questions raised in 1b.

3 Creative writing

On his first school day at Culver Creek, Miles gets up early to write a letter to his parents. Decide who or what he writes about and whether he tells them the whole truth. Then write his letter.

Pre-reading unit 2

1 Read the following quotes from unit 2 and speculate on forthcoming events or problems the protagonist Miles Halter and/or the other characters might have to face.

'... they pissed in my shoes.' • 'This teacher rocked.' • 'I'm unpredictable.' • 'The choice is yours. Both of you leave.'

© 2011 Cornelsen Verlag, Berlin. Alle Rechte vorbehalten.

Unit 2: Dr Hyde and the Smoking Hole

Summary – 'before'

In **the fourth chapter (pp. 33–38)**, Chip notices that the boys who played the prank on Miles also urinated into his (Chip's) shoes. He is furious and wants to find out why they are angry at him. Miles has his first French class with Mrs O'Malley and realizes that he will have to work hard at Culver Creek. He still feels a bit uncomfortable because he doesn't know many students yet. Miles shows Chip the three students who threw him into the lake. Miles also meets Dr Hyde, an elderly, rather frail teacher whom he likes immediately and whose class, World Religions, will concentrate on a topic important to Miles, the search for meaning. Unlike the other students, Miles spends his free time in his room reading where Alaska pays him a surprise visit to apologize for her behaviour the night before, explaining that she didn't know how bad it was.

In **the fifth chapter (pp. 38–42)**, Miles finds Chip in their room unsuccessfully trying to iron a shirt for a date with his girlfriend Sara. When Sara comes to pick Chip up, they argue about Chip's outfit and Sara leaves without Chip. Chip tells Miles that their relationship consists mostly of arguments and offers Miles a drink he calls ambrosia – a mixture of milk and vodka. Sara calls Chip later that evening to tell him that the Weekday Warriors think he reported Marya and Paul. Chip now knows why they urinated in his shoes and that the prank played on Miles was a punishment for being his roommate.

In **the sixth chapter (pp. 42–48)**, Miles is thrown out of Dr Hyde's class for looking out the window. Alaska sides with Miles and leaves too. Miles is upset because he is so fond of this teacher. After this incident Miles and Alaska wait for the others on the college green looking for four-leaf clovers. Miles is distracted by Alaska's body. After class, Chip and Takumi join them and they leave the college grounds to walk to a place in the woods close to the creek which they call 'the Smoking Hole'. Again, the conversation circles around the question as to who reported Marya and Paul. Alaska claims that it must have been one of the Weekday Warriors. Takumi creates a spontaneous rap and the others applaud him. When asked by Miles why Alaska smokes so much she says that she smokes to die.

Unit 2 ➢ Copymaster 5

NOTES

Make enough copies of copymaster 5 for students to work in groups of four or five. Cut out the twelve cards and put them in an envelope, one envelope for each group.

POSSIBLE ANSWERS

1 **'They pissed in my shoes.'** (p. 33. ll. 17–18):
The morning after Miles is thrown into the lake by three other students, Chip notices that the same boys must have urinated in his shoes. Chip wants to find out why they are angry at him and asks Miles to show him who it was.

2 **Madame O'Malley** (p. 34, ll. 4–11)
is Miles' strict French teacher. Miles realizes that he will have to work hard for good grades.

3 **search for meaning** (p. 36, l. 23):
When Miles meets Dr Hyde, he is fascinated by him because he hopes that his lessons on the three world religions will offer an answer to one of his most important questions – the way out of the labyrinth.

4 **ironing** (p. 38, ll. 8–14):
On Friday evening after the first week of school, Miles enters their room and finds Chip ironing a pink shirt. Chip does not know how to iron and finally puts the shirt on as wrinkled as it was.

5 **a movie star – a bitchy one** (p. 39, ll. 22–23):
This is how Miles describes Sara, Chip's girlfriend. She enters the room to pick up Chip, but makes a scene when she sees him in the wrinkled shirt. They argue and she leaves without him.

6 **ambrosia** (p. 40, l. 20):
This is the name Chip invented for a drink of milk with vodka. He puts the vodka into the milk so Mr Starnes won't find it. Though well-hidden, the mixture tastes like sour milk.

7 **edification and vocalized rambling** (p. 43, ll. 11 and 21):
Miles looks out of the window during Dr Hyde's class, musing on the interconnectedness of things. Dr Hyde admonishes Miles for failing to value his effort to educate him. Miles cannot explain his behaviour and is thrown out of class. Alaska leaves in protest.

8 **Miles Halter Fan Club** (p. 44, l. 17):
Miles is upset; he does not care if his fellow students don't like him (something he had gotten used to at his old school), but he does worry about the fact that Dr Hyde might not like him, since he has always been very popular among teachers.

9 **four-leaf clovers** (p. 44, l. 24):
After being thrown out of class, Alaska invites Miles to look for four-leaf clovers in the nearby meadow. While Alaska sits in the grass and leans forward to find what she is looking for, Miles feels strongly attracted to her and just looks at her.

10 an oasis (p. 46, l. 12):
After class, Alaska, Takumi, Chip and Miles leave the college grounds and show Miles a place in the woods they call the 'Smoking Hole'. Since it is near the river, equipped with some chairs and away from campus, Miles calls it 'an oasis'.

11 'You're adorable.' (p. 47, l. 18):
Alaska tells Miles that she pities him for what the three boys did to him and that she would have liked to kiss him. Thereupon Miles answers quick-wittedly that it is a shame she didn't do so, a remark Alaska finds adorable. She flirts with him and says that it is a shame she already has a boyfriend.

12 'I smoke to die.' (p. 48, l. 22):
Since Alaska smokes more than the boys, Miles asks her why. She tells him that while the others smoke to enjoy, she smokes to die.

Unit 2 ➤ Copymaster 6

POSSIBLE ANSWERS

1–2 Individual answers.

3 Dr Hyde as a teacher

facts	conclusions
has only one lung; has difficulties breathing; moves slowly	frail, sickly, weak
doesn't reveal his first name to students; asks them to call him by his title ('Dr Hyde'), not just 'Mr'	old-fashioned, conservative, demands respect
prefers an old-fashioned seating arrangement in his classroom; prefers lecturing to discussions	old-fashioned teaching methods
throws Miles out of his class because he looked out of the window and couldn't explain why	strict, authoritarian, uncompromising, asks students to be very attentive
expects students to abide by his rules and give him their undivided attention	uncompromising, strict, rigid
some of his students are afraid of him	authoritarian

4 Differing opinions

a *What Miles thinks:* Miles is fascinated by Dr Hyde's knowledge and by the subject he teaches ('World Religions'). He thinks Dr Hyde is great ('this teacher rocked', p. 36, l. 29), even a genius (p. 37, l. 30).
Reasons: In his class, Miles hopes to find the answer to 'The nature of the labyrinth […] and the way out of it' (p. 36, ll. 28–29). Although he is embarrassed when Dr Hyde throws him out of his class, he admits to not having listened and thinks he deserved to have been kicked out of class.

b *What Alaska thinks:* Alaska dislikes Dr Hyde's rigidness and tone and considers him condescending (p. 37, l. 29).
Reasons: Alaska is a rambunctious, rebellious girl who does not want to be told what to do. She dislikes Dr Hyde and his teaching methods (p. 44, ll. 2–3), calling him an 'asshole' (p. 44, l. 18) and a terrible teacher (p. 46, ll. 18–22).

c Their opinions differ as much as their characters. Miles the bookworm likes reading and studying. As an obedient student, he is used to his teachers liking him and feels guilty for not respecting Dr Hyde's rules. Alaska on the other hand is rebellious and does not care what others think about her. She likes playing pranks and breaking rules and therefore hates anyone as strict as Dr Hyde.

5 Now you
Individual answers.

ADDITIONAL/OPTIONAL TASKS

1 Imagine the following situation: Just after the new academic year has started Madame O'Malley and Dr Hyde meet in the staff room and talk about either Alaska or Miles. Choose one character and write down what the two teachers say. What do they think about their student?

2 Who do you think reported Marya and her boyfriend Paul? Take a vote in class.
a) Chip b) a Weekday Warrior c) Takumi
d) Sara e) Alaska
Write down the result of the vote and look at it again once you know who reported Paul and Marya.

TASKS

Work in groups of four or five. Take turns choosing a keyword and tell the others what you remember about its context. The others may add and/or correct information. Once all the cards have been taken, arrange them in chronological order. Then write a short summary of unit 2 and put it in your reading journal.

Madame O'Malley	ambrosia	ironing
a movie star – a bitchy one	edification and vocalized rambling	Miles Halter Fan Club
four-leaf clovers	an oasis	'You're adorable.'
'I smoke to die.'	search for meaning	'They pissed in my shoes.'

© 2011 Cornelsen Verlag, Berlin. Alle Rechte vorbehalten.

Unit 2 – Thinking about Teachers

TASKS

1 Role models

Name qualities you appreciate in a teacher and explain why. Are there teachers you would consider as role models? Give reasons.

2 Describing people

THINK: Look at the following list of adjectives. Which of them should a good teacher be? Check unknown words in a monolingual dictionary.
PAIR: With a partner, rank the adjectives from most important to least important.

ambitious • attractive • caring • demanding • elderly • experienced • friendly • funny • knowledgeable • lenient • middle-aged • modest • patient • quiet • self-confident • sociable • strict • trendy • unyielding • well-organized • wise • young • youthful

SHARE: Share your results with another pair or with the whole class.

3 Dr Hyde as a teacher

Collect all the information given on Dr Hyde and draw conclusions on his character and his personality as a teacher.

facts	conclusions

4 Differing opinions

a State what Miles thinks about Dr Hyde and explain why.

b State what Alaska thinks about Dr Hyde and explain why.

c Why do they have different opinions on this teacher?

5 Now you

Would like to have a teacher like Dr Hyde? Why or why not? Take into account what you found out in tasks **2** and **3**.

Pre-reading unit 3

In your reading journal, start a mind map of terms that you associate with friendship and of characteristics that you consider important in a friend.

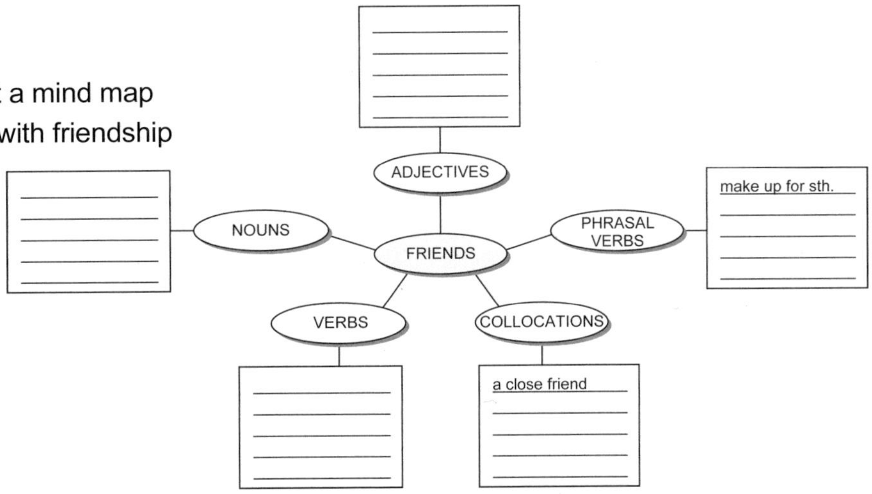

© 2011 Cornelsen Verlag, Berlin. Alle Rechte vorbehalten.

Unit 3: A Comet Needs a Tail

Summary – 'before'

Chapter 7 (pp. 48–54): Chip takes Miles to the first basketball game of the season. Although Miles hates everything to do with sports, he still accompanies Chip. Chip tells Miles that the Culver Creek team plays really badly and hardly ever wins a game. During the game Kevin, one of the boys who played the prank on Miles, approaches them, claims that Chip reported Marya and Paul, and offers a truce. Miles and Chip don't want a truce and make a bet which Kevin loses. Chip shouts abuse at the opposing team until the referee tells him to leave the gym. Miles follows him.

Chapter 8 (p. 53): Dr Hyde talks to Miles one day after class. He advises him to take the Buddhist belief of being truly present every minute of one's life more seriously.

Chapter 9 (pp. 54–56): Alaska takes a couple of students to McDonald's in her car to give them a lesson in precalculus because exams are ahead. On the way there, a girl called Lara sits on Miles's lap.

Chapter 10 (pp. 56–59): One day Alaska tells Miles that her parents let her choose her name when she was seven, so she looked at a globe and chose 'Alaska' because it was big and far from home. Only later did she discover the meaning of the word. She considers herself a good teacher and later wants to teach disabled children. While listening to her, Miles wants to kiss her. Again they talk about the labyrinth and how to escape it. Alaska thinks that thinking about the future is just an escape from the present.

Chapter 11 (pp. 59–60): 'The Eagle' catches Miles, Chip, Takumi and Alaska at the lake. Since Alaska and Chip were smoking, he orders the four of them to the Jury the next day to receive their punishment.

Chapter 12 (pp. 60–63): Told not to say anything in front of the Jury, Miles doesn't. Alaska is afraid because she has been caught smoking for the seventh time and doesn't want to disappoint her father. Chip and Alaska are given ten hours of doing dishes, whereas Takumi and Miles are let off.

Unit 3 ➤ Copymaster 7

NOTES

Copymaster 7 should be given as preparatory homework.

POSSIBLE ANSWERS

1 one hundred nine days before

- **a** Thinking that Chip reported Marya and Paul, Kevin takes revenge on Chip's roommate and thinks they are now even.
- **b** Chip knows about Miles's fascination with last words and thinks he's clever, so he proposes a bet: Kevin is to name an American president, and if Miles doesn't know his last words, there will be a truce; if he does, there won't. But Miles knows Millard Fillmore's last words, so there's no truce. In a way, they play a trick on Kevin, because he wouldn't have known the difference had Miles made up Fillmore's last words.
- **c** Chip knows that Culver Creek's basketball team has no chance of winning. He therefore shouts mean remarks at the opposing team to humiliate and annoy them. Since this is considered unfair, the referee expels him.
- **d** Miles would like to be as courageous and self-confident as Chip, but he isn't. So he makes use of a simile comparing Chip and himself to a comet and its tail. Like a comet wouldn't be visible without a tail, Chip needs someone like Miles as a follower and an audience; otherwise being what he is would be less rewarding.

2 one hundred eight days before

Dr Hyde is explaining the Buddhist belief that one should not only be *physically* present but also mentally present every moment of one's life and ready to absorb what is happening at that moment. When something is happening, there is therefore no room for thoughts about anything else (a concept linked to the practice of meditation).

3 one hundred one days before

- **a** The first important Maths test is approaching and Alaska offers to give some students a lesson at McDonald's in the lunch break.
- **b** For a whole hour Alaska eats fries, smokes and talks, explaining algebra. Her teaching methods do not differ greatly from Dr Hyde's whom she criticized for being condescending.

4 one hundred days before

- **a** Alaska's parents couldn't agree on a name for their daughter and allowed her to choose her name herself when she was seven years old. She looked at her father's globe and chose 'Alaska' because it was big and far from home. Later she found out that the word comes from the Aleut word *Alyeska* meaning 'that which the sea breaks against'. This would seem like a suitable name for someone who stands firm as a rock, which doesn't apply to Alaska: she seems restless and moody.

b *Possible answers:* Alaska just flirts with Miles but doesn't consider him a potential boyfriend; she wants to be faithful to Jake; she wants to play hard to get (see task **c**).

c This sentence can be seen as a pun. Alaska could either be saying that Miles will never become her boyfriend and/or that he will never understand her.

5 ninety-nine days before

Alaska regards being caught smoking as a minor incident (a battle) in a series of pranks they play or rules they break (the war). She seems very self-confident.

6 ninety-eight days before

a Miles is confused as to why he is told not to say anything. It would have been as easy for him to take the blame as it would have been to say that he wasn't smoking because he hadn't done anything, whereas Chip and Alaska already have a record of breaking the rules.

b Chip and Alaska want to teach Miles that honesty, loyalty and standing up for one another are important aspects of friendship.

c Mr Starnes possibly thinks Miles is privileged because his father already went to Culver Creek and there is less danger of him being expelled. Another possibility is that Mr Starnes considers being able to study at his school a privilege and wants to warn Miles, whom he likes, not to throw it away for something unimportant like smoking.

Unit 3 ➢ Copymaster 8

NOTES

The new texts about Alaska which the students agree on in their groups should be read out and discussed in class.

POSSIBLE ANSWERS

1 Thinking about Alaska

Individual answers.

2 Taking stock

a *Topics in the first three units:* labyrinth, life/death, love, friendship, loyalty/honesty

Unit 3 – Comprehension

TASKS

Please work on the following comprehension tasks. Make notes so that you can present your thoughts fluently in class.

1 one hundred nine days before (pp. 48–54)

- **a** Why does Kevin offer Miles and Chip a truce?
- **b** Explain how Miles and Chip avoid accepting the truce.
- **c** Why is Chip expelled from the gym?
- **d** Explain the sentence '… and they needed me, just like comets need tails.' (p. 54, ll. 9–10). Name the stylistic device the author uses here.

2 one hundred eight days before (p. 54)

In your own words, explain what Dr Hyde means by 'being truly present' (p. 54, l. 21).

3 one hundred one days before (pp. 54–56)

- **a** Why does Alaska ask Miles and some other students to go to McDonald's?
- **b** Describe how Alaska teaches the other students. What do you think of her teaching methods?

4 one hundred days before (pp. 56–59)

- **a** How did Alaska get her name? Explain whether or not you find the name 'Alaska' suitable for Alaska Young.
- **b** Speculate why Alaska does not kiss Miles.
- **c** Comment on the statement: 'You never get me. That's the whole point.' (p. 59, l. 6)

5 ninety-nine days before (pp. 59–60)

Explain the sentence in its context: 'Sometimes you lose a battle. But mischief always wins the war.' (p. 60, l. 26)

6 ninety-eight days before (pp. 60–63)

- **a** Describe Miles's feelings during the questioning. Why do you think Chip and Alaska tell Miles not to say a word?
- **b** Why does Mr Starnes ('the Eagle') warn Miles not to abuse his privileges? (p. 63, ll. 2–3)

© 2011 Cornelsen Verlag, Berlin. Alle Rechte vorbehalten.

Unit 3 – Read, Reflect, Rewrite

TASKS

1 Thinking about Alaska

Alaska is a selfish and arrogant girl. She is unreliable and doesn't care about others and their feelings. She is over-confident and lazy. She will surely fail at Culver Creek.

a THINK: Would you agree with this statement? Why or why not? If you don't agree, change single words to make the text acceptable for you.

b PAIR: Either explain the changes you made to your partner or explain why the statement does not have to be changed.

c SHARE: In groups of four or five, agree on a version of the statement and present it to the class.

2 Taking stock

a Make a list of topics dealt with in the first three units. Which of the topics interest you most? Give reasons.

b In your reading journal, start a new page for the topic 'friends' and note down what the characters say about friendship and/or what their actions reveal, e.g. whether friendship is important to them and if so, what is important to them in a friend.

c Then go back to the mind map on friends that you made as a pre-reading task for unit 3. Which of the things that were important to you are also important to the characters in the novel? Continue your mindmap on 'friends' as you read on.

Pre-reading unit 4

Speculate which of the topics you identified in **2a** will play a role in the following unit. Give reasons.

© 2011 Cornelsen Verlag, Berlin. Alle Rechte vorbehalten.

Unit 4: Girlfriends

Summary – 'before'

Chapter 13 (pp. 63–64): Alaska tells Miles that she has found him a girlfriend and planned a triple date for the upcoming weekend for herself and her boyfriend Jake, Chip and Sara, Miles and Lara, and Takumi.

Chapter 14 (pp. 65–70): At the weekend Miles meets Jake, Alaska's good-looking boyfriend, for the first time. Alaska kisses Jake in front of Miles and tells him that Jake is a good lover, making Miles envy Jake. The seven of them watch a basketball game at the gym. As usual, Chip provokes the opposing team and, as a result, Miles is hit hard by the ball. He has a concussion, vomits on Lara's jeans and is taken to hospital. Back at college, Chip tells Miles how Sara accused him of having had an erection for Alaska and then broke up with him.

Chapter 15 (pp. 71–72): It rains for days. Miles avoids talking to Lara about the embarrassing date. Alaska only makes rare appearances. When Miles tries talking to her in the cafeteria, she indicates that she does not want to answer any questions. He asks her if he has done something; she says no and walks away.

Chapter 16 (pp. 73–75): Dr Hyde gives the students the question for their final exam. Miles notices that Alaska has skipped Dr Hyde's class. When Chip and Miles meet her later she is outraged because some students flooded her room and many of her books are now seriously damaged. Chip promises to punish those responsible.

Chapter 17 (pp. 75–78): One day Takumi asks Miles to join him for a walk and tells him that Alaska was the one who reported Marya and Paul. Miles is shocked because he wouldn't have expected her to be disloyal, but now understands why Alaska took the blame at the Jury: she wanted to prove she could be trusted. Both boys agree that Chip must not learn the truth as he might have Alaska expelled for 'ratting'.

Chapter 18 (pp. 78–83): Alaska wakes Miles up early on a Saturday to persuade him to stay at Culver Creek with her over Thanksgiving. She has even prepared a list of reasons why Miles should stay. Miles calls his parents and lies to them, saying that he has exams to study for. His mother is disappointed and Miles has a bad conscience. Chip warns him not to start a relationship with Alaska, saying it would cause trouble. When Miles asks Alaska why she doesn't go home over Thanksgiving she says that she is afraid of ghosts.

Unit 4 ➢ Copymaster 9

NOTES

1 Who is it?
This task should be done as pair work. Students should do this off-the-cuff, i.e. the prompts should not accompany the reading process. Solutions should only be provided if students do not know the answer.

2 Direct and indirect characterization
This task may also be used to introduce the difference between direct and indirect characterization (for a definition of these terms, see copymaster 15).

3 Apologizing
This can be done as pair work. Results are presented to the class.

4 Now you
This task can be done as a follow-up activity and as homework.

5 Speculating
This can be done as pair- or group work. Students should be aware of the fact that Alaska is still a very enigmatic character and that the author reveals only very little about her, which is-another means of arousing curiosity and creating tension.

7 Life questions
If students have not yet completed task 4 (Life questions) of copymaster 1 (pre-reading), they should do so now in preparation for the essay; this can also be done as homework:
What is the most important question human beings must answer? Make notes. Read your questions to a partner. Note down his or her questions if you like them.
Brainstorming on the suggested questions may be done in a think-pair-share mode. All student speculations on Miles's essay topic should be collected and then compared to Miles's actual topic. Students should not be forced to read out their essays in front of the class because they may be very personal. Students can be encouraged to hand their essays in for personal feedback.

POSSIBLE ANSWERS

1 Who is it?

a *so. finds so. else a girlfriend:* Alaska tells Miles that she has found a girlfriend for him: Lara, the Romanian girl who sat on his lap on the way to McDonald's.

b *so. provokes so. else:* Chip provokes the star player of the opposing basketball team.

c *so. gets hurt:* Miles is hit by the basketball and has a concussion.

d *so. avoids talking to so. else:* Miles doesn't talk to Lara after the unsuccessful date.
e *so. is not very talkative:* Alaska doesn't want to talk to Miles when he meets her in the cafeteria.
f *so. may not live till the end of the school year:* Chip says he hopes Dr Hyde will live till the end of the school year because he is starting to enjoy his class.
g *so. pulls a prank on so. else:* some Weekday Warriors flood Alaska's room so that some of her best-loved books are damaged.
h *so. swears revenge:* Chip wants to take revenge on the students who flooded Alaska's room.
i *so. comes to a conclusion:* Takumi works out that Alaska reported Marya and Paul.
j *so. is terribly afraid of sth.:* Alaska is terribly afraid of being expelled (though the reader doesn't know why yet).
k *so. understands sth. in retrospect:* Miles understands why Alaska and Chip took the blame at the Jury to spare Takumi and himself: Alaska wanted to show she can be trusted and that friendship means loyalty.
l *so. persuades so. else to do sth.:* Alaska persuades Miles to stay at Culver Creek with her over Thanksgiving.
m *so. lies:* Miles lies to his parents saying that he has to study over Thanksgiving and can't come home.
n *so. warns so.:* Chip warns Miles against starting an affair with Alaska over Thanksgiving

2 Direct and indirect characterization

a mean; rude; bossy (indirect characterization)
b glamorous; bitchy (indirect characterization)
c condescending (indirect characterization)
d manipulative; deceitful (indirect characterization)
e mean; a bully (indirect characterization)
f arrogant; rude; sarcastic (direct characterization)

The author uses both direct and indirect means of characterizing Sara as unpleasant and unlikeable. She is the female counterpart of Chip who is likeable, loyal, helpful and upright.

3 Apologizing

Miles is still very embarrassed for vomiting on Lara. Students might argue that his reaction is understandable, but that it would have been better to talk to her instead of avoiding her.

4 Now you

a A matchmaker is someone who tries to arrange marriages or relationships between others.
b Individual answers.

5 Speculating

Alaska says that she is scared of ghosts and that her home is full of them (cf. p. 83, l. 31); something seems to be wrong with her family. A ghost is thought to be the spirit of a dead person or something that reminds people of the past. We don't know much about Alaska's family background. As a scholarship holder, she probably comes from a poor background. She mentions both parents twice only: once when she relates how she got her name (p. 57, ll. 4–19) and once when she tries to explain why she doesn't want to get expelled (p. 61, ll. 15–18).

6 Life questions

The most important question: What is the way out of the labyrinth?; Is the labyrinth living or dying?; What does it mean to be truly present?; The importance of friendship; Who I want to be; What people expect of me; Is there a life after death?; Making decisions; Living life to the full
What you might do if no one can help you answer this question: e.g. keep the question in your mind and make notes whenever something happens that may help or provide an answer; talk to as many people as possible about it; practise free writing
Free writing: Free writing is a pre-writing technique in which a person writes continuously for a certain amount of time without paying attention to spelling, grammar, or topic. It produces a kind of raw material and helps writers overcome a writer's block. Some people use this technique to collect initial thoughts and ideas on a topic, often as a first step to formal writing.

Unit 4 ➢ Copymaster 10
NOTES

1 Feelings

Students do the task on their own before discussing their results in class. This gives the teacher the opportunity to add synonyms or more precise alternative (cf. possible answers). Thus, students expand their vocabulary. The results should be kept in the reading journals.

POSSIBLE ANSWERS

1 Feelings

anxiety *(n)*, anxious *(adj)*: negative
confusion *(n)*, confused *(adj)*: negative
distress *(n)*, distraught *(adj)*: negative
discouragement *(n)*, discouraged *(adj)*: negative
elation *(n)*, elated *(adj)*: positive
enthusiasm *(n)*, enthusiastic *(adj)*: positive
exasperation *(n)*, exasperated *(adj)*: negative
excitement *(n)*, excited *(adj)*: positive
exhaustion *(n)*, exhausted *(adj)*: negative
frustration *(n)*, frustrated *(adj)*: negative

fury *(n)*, furious *(adj)*: negative
gratitude *(n)*, grateful *(adj)*: positive
guilt *(n)*, guilty *(adj)*: negative
hysteria *(n)*, hysterical *(adj)*: negative
infatuation *(n)*, infatuated *(adj)*: positive
intimidation *(n)*, intimidated *(adj)*: negative
jealousy *(n)*, jealous *(adj)*: negative
malice *(n)*, malicious *(adj)*: negative
misery *(n)*, miserable *(adj)*: negative
nervousness *(n)*, nervous *(adj)*: negative/neutral
outrage *(n)*, outraged *(adj)*: negative
offence *(n)*, offended *(adj)*: negative
pride *(n)*, proud *(adj)*: positive
restlessness *(n)*, restless *(adj)*: negative
seduction *(n)*, seductive *(adj)*: positive
shame *(n)*, ashamed *(adj)*: negative
stupefaction *(n)*, stupefied *(adj)*: neutral
temptation *(n)*, tempted *(adj)*: neutral

ADDITIONAL TASKS

Pre-reading unit 5

1 Which quote from task **2** might Alaska choose? Give reasons for your choice.

2 Alaska and Miles spend Thanksgiving together. They are alone on campus. What might happen? Collect a few ideas. Then work in groups of four and exchange your ideas. Decide on the three things that are most likely to happen. Explain why you think so.

Unit 4 ➢ Copymaster 11

NOTES

Copymaster 11 can be given to students who need help writing their essays.

Unit 4 – Life Questions

TASKS

1 Who is it?

Work with a partner. Using the following statements, take turns explaining what happens in unit 4.

- **a** someone finds someone a girlfriend
- **b** someone provokes someone
- **c** someone gets hurt
- **d** someone avoids talking to someone
- **e** someone is not very talkative
- **f** someone may not live till the end of the school year
- **g** someone pulls a prank on someone else
- **h** someone swears revenge
- **i** someone comes to a conclusion
- **j** someone is terribly afraid of something
- **k** someone understands something in retrospect
- **l** someone persuades someone to do something
- **m** someone lies
- **n** someone warns someone

2 Direct and indirect characterization

What do you think of Sara? Read the quotes below and find an adjective that best describes her in each situation. For each quote, decide whether it is an example of direct or indirect characterization.

- **a** 'Can't you at least press your shirt?' (p. 39, l. 18)
- **b** 'She looked like a movie star – a bitchy one.' (p. 39, ll. 22–23)
- **c** 'Chip, that chip on your shoulder makes you look even shorter.' (p. 39, l. 25)
- **d** 'Sara told Jake that I had a hard-on for Alaska.' (p. 39, l. 18)
- **e** 'She just likes bullying people.' (p. 39, l. 18)
- **f** 'Fine. Have a great night.' (p. 40, l. 6)

3 Apologizing

After the failed date, Miles does not talk to Lara. Why? Comment on his reaction, then write down what he could/should have said to her.

4 Now you

- **a** Look up the word *matchmaker* in a monolingual dictionary and explain it in your own words.
- **b** What do you think of matchmakers? State whether you have got any experience in matchmaking or in being matched up. Explain how you felt.

5 Speculating

Speculate on why Alaska is so afraid of being expelled.

6 Life questions

Choose the most important question you have and write Miles's essay for him. You don't have to know the answer to the question. You may want to include

- why this is the most important question for you,
- how you might go about finding an answer to it,
- what you might do if no one can help you answer it.

© 2011 Cornelsen Verlag, Berlin. Alle Rechte vorbehalten.

Unit 4 – Feelings Mind Map

TASKS

1 Feelings

Make a mind map or a list of the feelings the characters have in different situations. Add new feelings to your mind map as you read on.

Use different colours for positive and negative feelings. For each word, include the noun/verb/adjective/adverb as appropriate. Put the mind map into your reading journal.

Example:

negative	neutral	positive

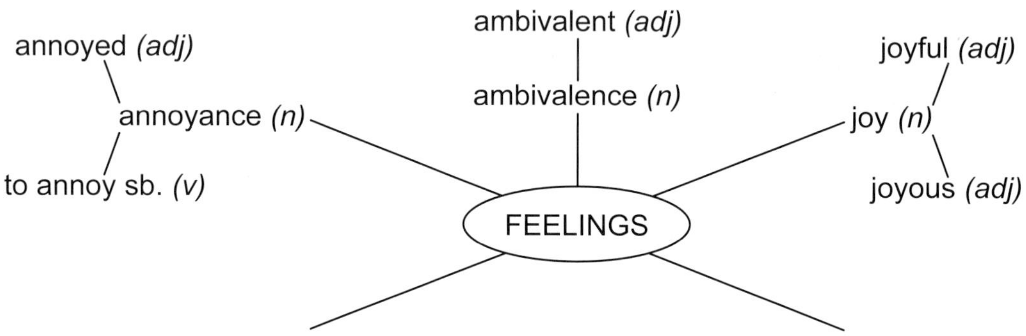

Pre-reading unit 5

1 Imagine you had to explain the word 'suffering' to a Martian who doesn't understand what it is. What would you say?

2 Read the following quotes carefully. Which quote do you agree with? Explain why.

'Pain is inevitable. Suffering is optional.' (without source)

'Have compassion for all beings, rich and poor alike; each has their suffering. Some suffer too much, others too little.' Buddha (c. 6th-5th century BC)

'We shall draw from the heart of suffering itself the means of inspiration and survival.'
Winston Churchill (1874–1965)

'To live is to suffer, to survive is to find some meaning in the suffering.'
Friedrich Nietzsche (1844–1900)

inevitable that you cannot avoid or prevent
compassion a strong feeling of sympathy for people who are suffering and a desire to help them
a means *(sing)* ein Mittel

3 What are the things that really make you suffer? Write them down and keep them in your reading journal.

© 2011 Cornelsen Verlag, Berlin. Alle Rechte vorbehalten.

Unit 4 – Working on Writing Tasks

TASKS

1 Planning ahead (10–15 minutes)

a Before you start, spend five minutes jotting down whatever comes to mind concerning the writing assignment.

b Circle the three most important (main) ideas and think about them in more detail. Find arguments or examples to support them.

c Put your main ideas in a convincing order. Consider which one you should you start with.

2 Introduction (5–10 minutes)

Think about how you want to begin. Consider what will grab the reader's attention the most:

- something funny?
- something mysterious?
- a question?
- a quote by a famous person?

Then formulate an introductory sentence.

3 Writing (20 minutes)

Write three paragraphs:

1 An introduction: Begin with a power-packed introductory sentence

2 A body: Write your main ideas or arguments and support them with examples (look back at **1 Planning ahead**). Write a paragraph about your main ideas.

3 A concluding paragraph: Give your final thoughts on the topic, e.g.: *All things considered, I like …*

4 Reviewing (5–10 minutes)

Re-read your text and check for spelling mistakes, linking words and general coherence.

Total time: 60 minutes

© 2011 Cornelsen Verlag, Berlin. Alle Rechte vorbehalten.

Unit 5: Thanksgiving

Summary – 'before'

Chapter 19 (pp. 84–86): After everyone has left, Alaska and Miles are alone on campus. Alaska shows Miles where she hides her wine. They spend the evening outside together. Alaska reads from Kurt Vonnegut's *Cat's Cradle* and puts her hand on Miles's leg. Miles is about to tell Alaska that he loves her when she interrupts him, saying that to her the labyrinth is all about suffering. When Miles wants to kiss her she stops him and asks him not to ruin it.

Chapter 20 (pp. 86–89): The next morning Alaska wakes Miles up. They enter Kevin's room, where they find a lot of haircare products. They leave the room through the window and go to the Smoking Hole.

Chapter 21 (pp. 89–92): Alaska invites Miles to go and search other students' rooms for porn movies. They find all sorts of things and Miles realizes that Alaska must have done this before. Finally they find a porn movie and watch it together. Alaska falls asleep on the couch and Miles is desperate to be close to her. He is fond of Alaska, but she seems out of his reach.

Chapter 22 (pp. 92–96): Alaska and Miles build a huge candle out of dripping wax in Alaska's room. Chip arrives at lunchtime and invites them to his home for Thanksgiving. They meet his mother, Dolores, who lives in a trailer park. Chip is ashamed of his poor home but proud of his mother who is an excellent cook. Chip has to sleep in a tent and Miles and Alaska share a bed.

Chapter 23 (pp. 96–97): On Thanksgiving Day everyone is in a good mood. They cherish the food and wine and list what they are thankful for.

Chapter 24 (pp. 97–99): Back at college, Alaska takes Miles to the liquor store where she always buys her wine and cigarettes with her fake ID card. She tells him about jokes her mother told her when she was little. Later that day she comes to see Miles in his room, crying. She tells him that she messes things up and that she is upset. Although he finds it hard to cope with Alaska's changing moods and does not really know what she is talking about, Miles still tries to console her.

Unit 5 ➢ Copymaster 12

NOTES

Copymaster 12 should be given to students before they read unit 5 so that they know what is expected of them. It may be done in pair- or group work.

Assign one of the two tasks to each student so that half of the class does task **1**, the other half task **2**. Alternatively, give students the following instructions:
Work with a partner and do the task assigned to you by your teacher. Then find two students who worked on the other task and exchange your results. You may help and correct each other.

POSSIBLE ANSWERS

1 Writing a summary

a 1) buried wine 2) porn movies 3) falling asleep 4) excellent cook 5) being thankful 6) fake ID 7) messing things up

b Alaska shows Miles where she <u>buries her wine</u> and reads to him from a novel. They search for <u>porn movies</u> and watch one together. Alaska <u>falls asleep</u> on the couch and Miles is desperate to be close to her. Chip invites them to his home for Thanksgiving. They meet his mother who is an <u>excellent cook</u>. They list what <u>they are thankful for</u>. Back at college Alaska takes Miles to the liquor store where she buys her wine with a <u>fake ID</u>. The same day she comes to Miles, crying. She tells him that she <u>messes things up</u>, which Miles does not understand.

2 Feelings

a *distress:* When Alaska comes to see Miles in his room she is distressed, saying she ruins everything (p. 99).
embarrassment: Miles is embarrassed when he sees how Chip and his mother live (p. 94/95); he is embarrassed when Alaska asks him whether the porn movie turns him on (p. 92, ll. 3–4).
gratitude: After the Thanksgiving dinner, everyone says what they're grateful for; Chip is especially grateful for his mother (p. 96).
incredulity: Miles is incredulous when Alaska shows him where and how she hides the bottles (p. 84) and at the fact that so many students keep alcohol hidden in their rooms (p. 90); see also unpredictability, pp. 86 and 87.
longing: After watching the porn movie with Alaska, Miles longs for her, but she seems out of his reach (p. 92).
moodiness: When Alaska comes into Miles's room sobbing, he tries to console her but at the same time finds her unpredictability and her changing moods annoying because he assumes that she does so intentionally (p. 98).

sensuality: Miles enjoys lying next to Alaska in the grass when she reads to him (p. 85) and sharing a bed with her (p. 96).
superiority: When they search the other students' rooms, Alaska tells Miles what to do and behaves in a rather bossy way (p. 87); when they watch the porn movie, Alaska gives Miles tips regarding sex (p. 91).
unpredictability: Lying in the grass with Alaska, Miles is just about to say that he loves her when she suddenly changes the topic and mentions the labyrinth (p. 86); on the second day of their Thanksgiving break Alaska wakes Miles up early to search the other students' rooms (p. 87); see also moodiness, p. 98

b Individual answers.

ADDITIONAL TASKS

2 Feelings

a Students can note down the adjectives corresponding to the nouns: distressed, embarrassed, grateful, incredulous, moody, longing, sensual, superior, unpredictable

Unit 5 ➢ Copymaster 13

NOTES

This is an optional copymaster which may also be used at some later point.

4a EXTRA **Doing research**

Edna St. Vincent Millay (1892–1950) was an American poet and writer, born in Maine. Her mother, a nurse, divorced her father (a school-teacher) in 1900 and encouraged independence in her daughter as well as a love of literature and music. Whilst at high school, Millay wrote for and served as editor in chief of the school magazine. She received a scholarship for Vassar College and, despite frequently breaking rules designed to protect female students, graduated with a B.A. in 1917. With little money, she moved to New York City, where she acted and had several love affairs. In 1919 she met Edmund Wilson, the managing editor of *Vanity Fair*, who published some of her work in 1920. In 1923, she became the first female winner of the Pulitzer Prize for poetry and married Eugen Jan Boissevain, a 43-year-old widower. They had no children. Her husband did all the household chores, travelled with her, encouraged her interests and even accepted her occasional love affairs with other people. In 1944 Millay had a nervous breakdown and was unable to write for two years. Millay died shortly after her husband's death in 1949, partly due to her excessive consumption of alcohol since the 1930s.

POSSIBLE ANSWERS

1–2

Individual answers.

3 Speculating

Possible answers: Alaska might choose quote A because she also lives her life to the full. She does not seem to care about the consequences of what she does (p. 56, ll. 22–23).
She might choose quote B because this is how she might feel when she thinks of her mother.
She might choose quote C because it strikes a chord with her. She quotes it herself (p. 92, l. 30) and links it to depression – night falls fast on everything and the present is not seen positively.
She might choose quote D because she is not interested in religion and does not like Dr Hyde's class.

4 EXTRA **Doing research**

b Edna St. Vincent Millay is Alaska's hero (p. 93, l. 7) because there are many similarities between Alaska's and the poet's life. Edna St. Vincent Millay lived a very bohemian lifestyle and had many lovers even after she married. She was rather whimsical, psychologically fragile, drank a lot and fought for women's rights.

ADDITIONAL TASKS

1. Re-read p. 85, l. 8 – p. 86, l. 21. Imagine you are a grasshopper sitting on Alaska's knee. Unfortunately, you are not able to understand what human beings say, but you can interpret their body language because grasshoppers are very sensitive creatures. Describe what you see as accurately as possible.
2. Re-read p. 92, ll. 16–18. Then complete the following poem Miles writes about Alaska.
   Alaska
   If people were colours, I was … and she was …
   If people were animals, I was … and she was …
   If people were sounds, I was … and she was …
   If people were food, I was … and she was …
   If people were smells, I was … and she was …
   If people were music, I was … and she was …
   (Students may add more ideas.)

➤ Copymaster 12 | Unit 5 – Comprehension

TASKS

Work on the task assigned to you; both tasks apply to the whole unit (pp. 84–99).

1 Writing a summary

a Look at the list of key words from the unit and put them in the correct order.

> being thankful • buried wine • excellent cook • fake ID • falling asleep • porn movies • messing things up

b Use the words to write a short summary of the unit (no more than 100 words).

2 Feelings

a Look at the words below. Make sure you know what each word means (use a monolingual dictionary if necessary). Which event or situation in unit 5 might each word best describe? Give reasons.

> distress • embarrassment • gratitude • incredulity • longing • moodiness • sensuality • superiority • unpredictability

2b Add two more feelings to the list and ask your partner to find a situation in the unit that each word describes best.

✂ ---

Work on the task assigned to you; both tasks apply to the whole unit (pp. 84–99).

1 Writing a summary

a Look at the list of key words from the unit and put them in the correct order.

> being thankful • buried wine • excellent cook • fake ID • falling asleep • porn movies • messing things up

b Use the words to write a short summary of the unit (no more than 100 words).

2 Feelings

a Look at the words below. Make sure you know what each word means (use a monolingual dictionary if necessary). Which event or situation in unit 5 might each word best describe? Give reasons.

> distress • embarrassment • gratitude • incredulity • longing • moodiness • sensuality • superiority • unpredictability

b Add two more feelings to the list and ask your partner to find a situation in the unit that each word describes best.

© 2011 Cornelsen Verlag, Berlin. Alle Rechte vorbehalten.

Edna St. Vincent Millay (1892–1950)

A

My candle burns at both ends
It will not last the night;
But ah, my foes, and oh, my friends –
It gives a lovely light.

From: 'First Fig', in: *A Few Figs from Thistles*, Harper, 1920

B

Where you used to be, there is a hole in the world, which I find myself constantly walking around in the daytime, and falling into at night. I miss you like hell.

From: *Letters*, Harper, 1952

C

Night falls fast. Today is in the past.

From: 'Not So Far as the Forest', in: *Huntsman, What Quarry?*, Harper,1939

D

There is no God. But it does not matter. Man is enough.

From: *Conversation at Midnight*, Harper,1937

1 burn the candle at both ends become very tired from trying to do too many things and sleeping too little
3 foe enemy

TASKS

1 In your own words

Read the four quotes carefully. Make sure you understand them, then rephrase them in your own words.

2 Making a choice

Which quote do you like best? Why? Discuss your reasons with a partner.

3 Speculating

Which quote could be Alaska's favourite quote and why?

4 EXTRA Doing research

a Do some research on Edna St. Vincent Millay and prepare a short presentation.

b Why is she Alaska's hero? Write a comment and put it in your reading journal.

Pre-reading unit 6

Miles writes a letter to his parents after the Thanksgiving break at the end of November, telling them that he is looking forward to coming home over Christmas. What is he looking forward to? Write his letter for him and put it in your reading journal.

© 2011 Cornelsen Verlag, Berlin. Alle Rechte vorbehalten.

Unit 6: Pulling a Prank

Summary – 'before'

Chapter 25 (pp. 99–101): All students go home for Christmas. Miles studies a lot for his exams and enjoys being with his parents.

Chapter 26 (pp. 101–103): After the Christmas break Alaska suggests they pull a prank to take revenge on Kevin and his friends. Miles is annoyed as he is left out when Chip and Alaska plan the prank. He tells himself that he shouldn't care so much about Alaska.

Chapter 27 (pp. 103–104): While Chip and Alaska are planning the prank, Miles prepares for his exams and even manages to finish his religion essay, concluding with an answer to why people believe in life after death.

Chapter 28 (pp. 104–114): After the exams, Miles, Takumi, Lara, Chip and Alaska set out to pull the prank. All of them pretend to spend the weekend off the school campus for different reasons. They secretly meet at the barn and Chip reads out the plan before they put it into action: Miles and Takumi light firecrackers to lure Mr Starnes out of his house and distract him. At the same time, Lara puts blue dye in some boys' haircare products, while Chip and Alaska use Mr Starnes's computer to send out reports to some parents saying that their children have failed classes. Everything goes well and they all meet back at the barn and sleep there.

Unit 6 ➢ Copymaster 14

NOTES

If the teacher wants students to write a summary of all chapters, a jigsaw puzzle could be used as a time-saving way of summarizing chapters 25–27, as they are of similar length. The teacher divides the class into three groups. Each group reads one of the three chapters. In pairs, students make sure they understand what they've read. Individually they write a summary of the chapter assigned to them and put it in their reading journal. Students then work in expert groups of three, each as representative of one chapter, and read their summaries to each other. The other two students note down this summary.

1 Who could have thought this?

This task may be done in pair- or group work. It is to help the students summarize the content of this chapter and prepare them for task **2**. There may be more than one possible answer.

An alternative, quicker way of checking students' comprehension is to give them the following questions (one each for chapters 25–27, two for chapter 28):

1. Summarize how Miles feels during the Christmas break. Why is he happy to have a family? (p. 100 l. 31)
2. Explain the sentence '*You don't* have *to care about her*, I told myself. *Screw her.*' (p. 103, ll. 4–5)
3. Which question does Miles answer in his religion paper? Summarize his answer. Would you agree with what he says?
4. What are the different tasks Takumi, Lara, Miles and Alaska are given by Chip?
5. Explain Chip's annoyance at Alaska's decision to send out more than the agreed number of progress reports.

2 Who is telling the story?

Before working on **2a** students may name what they know about the terms author / narrator / point of view. Then copymaster 15 can be handed out and read together in class. **2b** and **2c** should be done individually or given as homework. Alternatively, the teacher can give students copymaster 15 as preparatory homework for task **2a**.

2d Students work in groups of four, read their texts to each other and discuss the effect the different narrators/perspectives have.

2e The reader sees everything through Miles's eyes and therefore tends to identify with him and share his opinion on other characters and events. He is a likeable character which is why the reader tends to trust him.

3 Being invincible

a–c may be answered/discussed by the whole class.

d may be discussed in small groups or given as homework so that students can work individually without having to share anything with anybody.

POSSIBLE ANSWERS

1 Who could have thought this?

- **a** Miles might have thought this while at home for Christmas.
- **b** Chip might have thought this when Miles is impressed by his memory.
- **c** Mr Starnes could have thought this when Chip, Miles and Takumi tell him that they are going to spend the weekend at Chip's.
- **d** Chip's mother could have thought this when he asked her to lie for him saying that he'll be spending the weekend with her.
- **e** Miles/Lara/Takumi could have thought this when Chip explains the prank.

- **f** Lara could have thought this when looking for Kevin's hair gel into which she is supposed to put the blue dye.
- **g** Chip could have thought this after entering Mr Starnes's office and trying to log into the school computer.
- **h** Mr Starnes could have thought this when he hears more and more firecrackers exploding in the vicinity of the college.
- **i** Alaska could have thought this when Chip ran out because he had heard a noise.
- **j** Chip could have thought this when he re-entered the office and found Alaska printing out progress reports for another 23 students although their plan had been different. Miles could also have thought this when Alaska tells the others about this.
- **k** Miles could have thought this when Alaska is full of malicious glee at the thought of Kevin's blue hair.
- **l** Miles/Lara/Takumi could have thought this while sitting together in the barn talking about what they had just accomplished.

2 Who is telling the story?

- **a** Miles tells the story. He is a first-person narrator. His point of view is limited.
- **b** *Model answer Lara:* I am so proud to be in on this! My job is easy, I just have to sneak into Kevin's room and find the bottle of gel. Here we are. The door is open – thank God! I'm the only one to be working alone, all the others are working in pairs. I wish I was with Pudge; I really like him and I hope I get a chance to kiss him tonight. Maybe I can even sleep in his sleeping bag with him. Now where is the gel? Chip said it was … Ah, here it is. OK now, careful with the dye, no spots anywhere, that's what Chip told me. OK, here we go. A little more blue … Ha! Ha! Kevin will look really nice! There is someone in the hall, shit, what am I going to do now? Phew, that was close. Gel back into the cupboard, out of the room. Time for the next one. How much time have I got left? OK, everything is fine.
- **c** The five of them were sitting in the barn talking to each other. They were in a good mood, laughing and giggling. Alaska talked a lot about how annoyed Kevin would be when he discovered he had dyed his own hair. Miles just watched her, unable to understand why she hated the other students so much. When he was about to ask her, she lay down behind some piles of hay and fell asleep in an instant. Knowing her well, the others did not try to wake her up.
- **d–e** Individual answers.

3 Being invincible

- **a** Miles is excited to be allowed to take part in the prank. He feels strong and is sure that nothing can happen to him and Takumi. He feels invincible because he is happy. He has finally found some real friends and has gained self-confidence.
- **b** In this context, the 'Great Perhaps' might imply adventure; being part of a group; being accepted; having friends; sharing experiences; breaking rules together;
  breaking out of his former role (the skinny boy who reads a lot and has no friends); freedom; change.
- **c** The Marines are an elite unit of the US army and considered the best soldiers. Miles and Takumi think they play the most important part in the prank because they have to distract Mr Starnes so that Chip, Alaska and Lara can each do their part.
- **d** Individual answers.

ADDITIONAL TASKS

1. Why do Chip and Alaska exclude Miles from their planning activities? Collect some ideas.
2. Do either **a** or **b**, then read out your dialogues. What do the dialogues tell you about the characters?
   - **a** Write a dialogue in which Chip tries to convince Alaska to include Miles in their planning activities.
   - **b** Write a dialogue in which Alaska tries to convince Chip to include Miles in their planning activities.
3. What do the characters look like? Go through magazines or surf the Net for pictures of Miles, Takumi, Lara, Alaska and Chip. Justify your choice. In groups, decide on one picture for each character. Keep the picture; you will need it later on.

Unit 6 – The Narrator

TASKS

1 Who could have thought this?

Work with a partner to find out who could have thought the following and describe the situation they were in at the time.

- **a** I'm a lucky boy.
- **b** How nice to have someone admire my memory.
- **c** All three of them? Hm, maybe I should check this with Mrs Martin …
- **d** I wonder what he's up to.
- **e** This guy is really clever.
- **f** Where's the gel? Chip said it was … Ah, here it is.
- **g** OK, here we go, the password, quick! Shit! Calm down, try again. Yes, that's it!
- **h** They're in trouble, whoever they are. What an impudence!
- **i** What if I send out some more progress reports? Yes, that's it!
- **j** Why does she always have to do what *she* wants?
- **k** Why does she hate them so much?
- **l** I'm so glad I came here.

2 Who is telling the story?

- **a** Based on the information in copymaster 15, describe the narrator chosen by John Green to tell his story.
- **b** We only learn what happens to Miles and Takumi. Retell the prank from either Lara, Alaska or Chip's point of view.
- **c** Retell the final scene in the barn (p. 112, l. 4 – p. 114, l. 26) from a third-person omniscient point of view. Your text should be shorter than the passage in the book, focusing on what actually happens.
- **d** Read your texts to each other. What effect does the point of view have on you, the reader?
- **e** Speculate why John Green chose Miles to be his narrator.

3 Being invincible

- **a** 'I'd never felt cooler. The Great Perhaps was upon us, and we were invincible. The plan may have had its faults, but we did not' (p. 107, ll. 3–5). Explain Miles's thoughts in your own words. Why does he feel invincible?
- **b** What could the 'Great Perhaps' be in this context?
- **c** Why do Miles and Takumi compare themselves to Marines?
- **d** Do you remember a moment in your life when you felt invincible? Make notes and put them in your reading journal or share your ideas with a partner or in a group.

Pre-reading unit 7

Which was the worst day in your life so far? What was the best day in your life so far? Make notes and keep them in your reading journal.

© 2011 Cornelsen Verlag, Berlin. Alle Rechte vorbehalten.

Point of View

The point of view of a narrative is the perspective from which the story is told. The point of view of a first-person narrator is easy to identify: the narrator tells the story from his or her own perspective. However, a third-person narrator can also tell a story from a character's point of view by focusing on what that character can see, hear and maybe even think.

The concepts of **narrator** and **point of view** are closely related:

A first-person narrator can only have

→ **a limited point of view:** A character in the story can't possibly know everything that's going on. The reader's view is limited by what the character sees and wants to tell.

A third-person narrator can have

→ **a limited point of view:** The narrator may be limited to the experience of one or more characters in the story, or maybe he or she doesn't know the characters thoughts and feelings.

→ **an unlimited point of view:** This omniscient narrator doesn't follow any one character, but moves around, entering into characters' minds whenever he or she wants.

Characterization

Characterization is the way in which the author of a fictional text presents his or her characters to the reader or, in the case of a play or film, to the audience. There are two main ways of presenting a character:

- direct characterization ('telling')
  Somebody tells the reader what sort of person a character is. This can be:
  – the narrator
  – another character in the story
  – the character him- or herself
- indirect characterization ('showing')
  The reader has to draw conclusions about a character based on what the character says and does.

Language help

- … is shown/presented/characterized as somebody who …
- … is characterized by his/her actions/speech which …

© 2011 Cornelsen Verlag, Berlin. Alle Rechte vorbehalten.

Unit 7: To Be Continued?

Summary – 'before'

Chapter 29 (pp. 114–126): The next morning they have a freestyle rap contest. As usual, Takumi wins. In the afternoon Alaska says it's time to get drunk. She asks everybody to tell the others about the best and the worst days in their lives. Only the winner of each round does not have to drink. They learn that Alaska lost her mother when she was a small child. Miles finally understands that this incident had a crucial influence on Alaska and the way she acts and behaves. In the end they are all quite drunk and Miles kisses Lara, with whom he shares a sleeping bag. For Miles this was the best day of his life.

Chapter 30 (pp. 126–127): Early the next morning Chip wakes the others up. They are all hung-over and walk back to the campus. When Miles tells Alaska that she shouldn't drink so much, she tells him that she is a deeply unhappy person. They check in with Mr Starnes, who does not seem to suspect anything, go back to their rooms and sleep.

Chapter 31 (pp. 127–135): The next morning Kevin enters Miles and Chip's room. His hair is blue and he offers a truce which Chip refuses. Miles spends the afternoon with Lara and she offers to perform oral sex on him. Since neither of them knows how to do it, they ask Alaska for help. They try again and Miles has his first orgasm with a girl. Miles spends the evening with Chip and Alaska. Alaska flirts with Miles and seduces him; they kiss and both fall asleep. The phone rings. When she returns from the phone, Alaska insists she has to leave. Miles and Chip distract Mr Starnes and Alaska drives off although she is drunk.

Unit 7 ➤ Copymaster 16

NOTES

If the students are slow readers, they may read chapter 31 at home before doing the cooperative reading tasks in class. Groups are formed depending on the number of students in class: in large courses, students form groups of five, in smaller courses, they form groups of four. In the latter case, one student does both C and D.

POSSIBLE ANSWERS

1 **Working individually**

Student A – Formulating questions: Why does Chip not accept Kevin's peace offer?; Why does Miles like last words?; Why do you think Miles does not know how to talk to Lara (p. 131, ll. 22–23)?; Why does Chip think that 'this will end poorly' (p. 134, l. 13) when he realizes Alaska and Miles are making out?; Why do you think Chip and Miles help Alaska leave campus?

Student B – Summarizing: See the summary of chapter 31 above.

Student C – Describing Miles: p. 128, l. 20: Miles tries to calm down Chip who throws a can at Kevin (he is conciliatory);
p. 131, l. 23: Miles is frustrated that he doesn't know how to talk to Lara (he is thoughtful, deep);
p. 133, l. 10 – p. 134, l. 5: Miles makes out with Alaska although he knows she has a boyfriend (he is enamoured, infatuated);
p. 133, l. 10 – p. 134, l. 5: He makes out with Alaska although he has a girlfriend (he is disloyal).

Student D – Describing Alaska: p. 131, l. 33: Alaska offers to give Chip a 'pity blow' (she is cheeky);
p. 133, l. 10 – p. 134, l. 5: she plays with Miles and his feelings for her: first she flirts with Miles, then she asks him and Chip to help her leave the campus in the middle of the night (she is unpredictable, moody);
p. 133, l. 10 – p. 134, l. 5: Alaska seduces Miles although she has a boyfriend (she is disloyal)

Student E – Predicting: The relationship between Miles and Lara will not last, it seems to be a purely physical relationship; Miles doesn't know how to talk to Lara (p. 131, ll. 22–23).
Something is going to happen to Alaska (p. 134, l. 30): 'equal in our guilt' and p. 135, ll. 4–9: the questions Miles and Chip did not ask, may be seen as clues.
Something has happened either to Jake or to someone else Alaska knows, making her wants to leave immediately (p. 134, ll. 16–18).
The relationship between Alaska and Miles will not end happily. Clues: Chip's warning (p. 133, l. 27–28) and his prediction 'This is going to end poorly' (p. 134, l. 13).
Chip is going to get into trouble when the Weekday Warriors get their (fake) progress reports.

2 **Pooling results**

Individual answers

Unit 7 ➤ Copymaster 17/18

NOTES

If appropriate, the crossword can be done in the same groups of four as the reciprocal reading activity (copymaster 16).

POSSIBLE ANSWERS

Cooperative crossword

1 r**h**yme (p. 116)
2 best **d**ay / worst **d**ay (p. 117)
3 han**g**over (p. 127)
4 phone ca**l**l (p. 134)
5 l**o**ss (p. 122)
6 make **out** (p. 133–134)
7 mysteriou**s** (p. 118)
8 pre-pra**n**k (p. 101)
9 gu**i**lt (p. 134)
10 humiliat**i**on (p. 120)
Solution: 'hiding out loud' (p. 115)

Unit 7 ➢ Copymaster 19

NOTES

As a means of differentiation, the teacher may ask better students – one representative of each role – to come up front and improvise a version of the role-play. In weaker courses, the teacher gives students time to prepare the role-play. Alternatively, the role-play can be done when the whole novel has been read, i.e. at the end of unit 12.

ADDITIONAL TASKS

1 Labelling a picture

Imagine the scene in which the five adolescents sit together and tell each other about the best and the worst days in their lives. Make a short sketch of the scene. Your teacher will dictate some words to you. Then write the words you consider relevant (i.e. not necessarily all words) in the appropriate spot in your drawing. Work with a partner. Show him or her your drawing and explain why you put which word in which place.

Before the dictation, the teacher makes sure the students know the meaning of the dictated words.

Words to be dictated: comfortable, warm, away from others, soft, bright, cosy, old, hidden, round, slippery, away, alone, exciting, high, delicate, oppressed, secure, imaginative, blue, red, intimate, relaxed, dreamy, light, noisy, open, under, early, dangerous, cold, forbidden, with, out of sight, clear, hard to reach, quick, new, colourful, sleepy, exciting, daring, pleasant/unpleasant, strong/weak

After partners have exchanged their results, one or two students may present their result in class (optional).

2 The last day

a Reread Miles's encounter with Lara (p. 128, l. 22 – p. 131, l. 24), then comment on it. Would you agree with Miles's depiction of the encounter as 'the fellatio fiasco' (p. 131, ll. 26–27)? Explain why or why not.

b Reread Miles's encounter with Alaska (p. 132, l. 4 – p. 134, l. 13), then comment on it.

c With a partner, compare the two scenes and discuss reasons why they come so close together. Then explain the effect of the juxtaposition of the two scenes.

Note: If students notice the fact that the girl 'brazen' (p. 129, l. 12) enough to offer Miles a blow job is not American (but Romanian), the teacher may discuss examples of prejudice against foreigners (or at least Eastern Europeans and Asians) in *Looking for Alaska.* Another example might be the description of Takumi's eating habits (p. 26, ll. 32–33; p. 174, l. 24). Students may bring up criticism at this opportunity or in the context of the role-play (➢ copymaster 18).

3 Pre-reading unit 8 ('after')

The teacher may collect the predictions that were made in the different groups on the board or on an overhead transparency (➢ copymaster 16, student E). Once the students have read unit 8, they can then compare their speculations with what actually happens in the novel.

Unit 7 – Reciprocal Reading: The Last Day

NOTE

Read the chapter 'the last day' (pp. 127–135) carefully. The annotations will help you to understand difficult words. Then get into groups of five (A–E).

Read your assignment and take notes according to your task. Ask your group members for words you don't understand but consider essential for the understanding of the excerpt. Then do your task.

TASKS

1 Working individually

Student A – Formulating questions

Formulate five comprehension questions for the other group members. Avoid questions with one-word answers.

Student B – Summarizing

In no more than 5–7 sentences, write a summary of the chapter.

Student C – Describing Miles

Note down passages that tell us something about Miles. Find adjectives that characterize him.

Student D – Describing Alaska

Note down passages that tell us something about Alaska. Find adjectives that characterize her.

Student E – Predicting

What will happen next? Make some predictions based on what you have read in this chapter.

2 Pooling results

After you have worked on your task, share your results with your group. Bear in mind the following questions:

- **a** Has student A covered the most important information?
- **b** Has student B summarized the chapter adequately, focusing on the most important information?
- **c** Have students C and D found passages that tell us something about Miles/Alaska?
- **d** Has student E made plausible predictions? Give reasons.

© 2011 Cornelsen Verlag, Berlin. Alle Rechte vorbehalten.

Unit 7 – Cooperative Crossword (1)

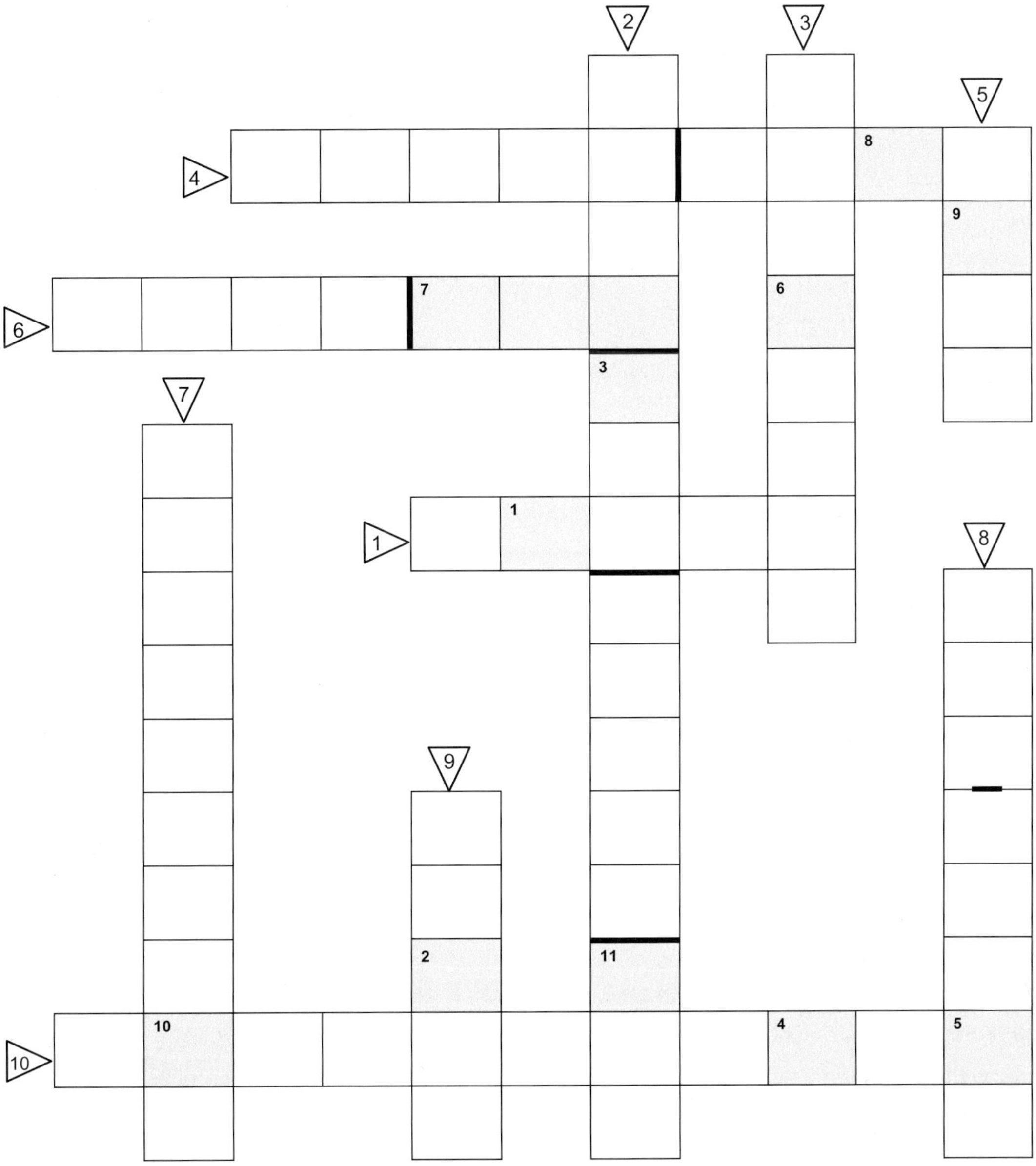

TASK

How does Miles describe what Alaska, Chip, Takumi, Lara and he are doing in unit 7? To find out, fill in the blanks below with the letters in the marked and numbered boxes.

SOLUTION

__ __ __ __ __ __   __ __ __   __ __ __ __

1 2 3 4 5 6   7   8 9 10 11

© 2011 Cornelsen Verlag, Berlin. Alle Rechte vorbehalten.

Unit 7 – Cooperative Crossword (2)

NOTE

Work in groups of four. There are four clues per answer; each group member receives a different clue for each answer. Only if you work together will you find the solution. Where the answer consists of more than one word, this is shown in parentheses.

CLUES

Student A

1 You need it to rap.
2 It includes two superlatives (four words).
3 an unpleasant feeling
4 the apparent cause for Alaska's sudden departure on her last night (two words)
5 The ~ of her mother had a great impact on Alaska.
6 petting (two words)
7 Miles thinks Alaska *wants* to appear ~.
8 Chip remembers the last one which was in 1987 (two words).
9 an unhappy feeling caused by thinking you have done something wrong
10 a noun

Student B

1 Some poems ~.
2 the name of the game they play (four words)
3 caused by too much alcohol
4 When you receive or make a ~ you speak to someone (two words).
5 'Death' is a synonym of ~ in this sense.
6 to kiss and touch each other (two words)
7 an adjective
8 The answer has a prefix (two words).
9 Alaska has feelings of ~ for not dialling 911.
10 It has five syllables.

Student C

1 'Zoo' and 'bear' don't ~.
2 For Alaska, the two opposites refer to two consecutive days (four words).
3 You usually try to sleep it off.
4 A ~ (or the absence of one) already played an important role in Alaska's life (two words).
5 The opposite of another meaning of ~ is 'profit'.
6 What Miles and Alaska do on Alaska's last night (two words).
7 puzzling
8 This comes before another, similar event (two words).
9 Miles finds Chip and himself 'equal in their ~' for having helped Alaska leave.
10 Being kicked out of class may cause you to feel this.

Student D

1 'Zoo' and 'gnu' ~.
2 It contrasts two words (four words).
3 It gives you a headache.
4 The ~ arrived in the hall because mobile phones aren't allowed on campus (two words).
5 The ~ of a loved one is hard to bear.
6 a phrasal verb; American English (two words)
7 Someone who is ~ makes you want to know more about him or her.
8 Planned and executed in unit 6, Alaska, Miles, Chip and Lara reap the fruits of their ~ (two words) in unit 7.
9 Her feelings of ~ may have caused Alaska's death.
10 shame

© 2011 Cornelsen Verlag, Berlin. Alle Rechte vorbehalten.

Unit 7 – A Role-Play

TASKS

1 Choose one of the six characters below. Get together with classmates who chose the same character. In your group, collect arguments for your character. You may use the language help below to help you formulate the arguments.

2 Form groups of six so that each character is represented once and exchange your arguments. Practise doing the role-play; volunteers may perform it in front of the class.

Mr/Mrs Worrywart (a parent)
Your son/daughter has told you about the novel he/she is reading in her English lessons. You are shocked that the teacher has chosen a book in which words like 'blow job', 'sex', 'orgasm' and 'porn movies' come up. And the main character – Alaska – could never be a role model for your child since she drinks, smokes and shows signs of rude behaviour. Actually, your son/daughter quite enjoys reading the novel and so do most of the other students in class. You have been invited to school to discuss the matter and you want to convince the teacher, the head teacher and the other students that this book should not be read in class. Voice your concerns!

Blushy (a student)
You are a very shy student and do not enjoy reading *Looking for Alaska* at all. You do not understand why everybody in your class thinks Alaska is cool. You think she is rude, moody and ill-mannered. That's why you can't identify with Miles, either. Why is he so mad about her? You are an avid reader, you like your teacher a lot and you always do your homework, but you don't want to talk about sex in school.

Smiley (a student)
You are a very self-confident student and enjoy reading *Looking for Alaska*: a great book with authentic characters, teen language, and a bit of juicy stuff, too. Not like some books you have to read for school which want to teach you something and make you a better person. You do not understand the mother's worries.

Mr/Mrs Rotaidem (a social worker)
You try to understand everybody's worries and concerns. You want to make sure that everybody can say what they think without hurting anybody else. You are worried about Blushy, because he/she might be too shy to take part in the discussion so you try to encourage him/her to express her feelings.

Mr/Mrs Rock (a teacher)
You are a very experienced teacher. You have chosen *Looking for Alaska* because you think it is a good book on topics that your students will identify with. Your impression is that most students in your class like the book. You don't really want parents to interfere with your decisions, yet you are polite and want to convince the mother of the fact that you have the students' interests in mind.

Mr/Mrs Headway (the head teacher)
You are the head teacher of the school. You like the English teacher (Mr/Mrs Rock) because he/she does a good job. However, you take parents' complaints seriously and are worried about the reputation of your school / the English department. Your aim is to reach a compromise.

Language help
I think/suppose/guess/... • In my opinion / If you ask me • I quite agree with … because …. • What I am trying to say is … • I take your point, but … • On the contrary • I disagree / don't agree … • I see what you mean, but I don't believe/think that … • Did you really mean to say that … ?

© 2011 Cornelsen Verlag, Berlin. Alle Rechte vorbehalten.

Unit 8: Straight and Fast

Summary – 'after'

Chapter 32 (pp. 139–145): The next morning Mr Starnes wakes up all the students and asks them to come to the gym. Miles notices that Alaska is not among the crowd. In tears, Mr Starnes tells them that Alaska was killed in an accident the night before. Everyone is shocked and Miles feels guilty. Incredulous, he assumes that this might be another trick Alaska is playing on them until Mr Starnes tells him that he saw Alaska and that her car had hit a police car. Walking back to his room, Miles is aware of the fact that he will never know what Alaska's last words were.

Chapter 33 (pp. 145–149): Miles can't sleep all night and is tormented by the feeling of loss. Chip tries to distract himself by learning things by heart. All of a sudden he leaves the room with his almanac. Miles wonders whether he had mattered to Alaska at all and whether she had wanted to go and see Jake that night. Lara comes to talk to him but he doesn't want to talk to her. He has a nightmare and is all alone because Chip hasn't returned.

Chapter 34 (pp. 149–151): Two days later Chip returns at five a.m., freezing because he has walked eighty-two miles without a break. He tells Miles that he had been fed up with Alaska's moods.

Chapter 35 (pp. 151–153): On Sunday all students attend Alaska's funeral. Takumi, Lara, Chip and Miles go by car, avoiding the spot where Alaska died. On the way to the funeral Miles is in tears at the idea that Alaska might have loved him back. Though he had hoped to see her again he finds the casket closed. Alaska's father tells him that she had wanted it to be that way. Chip and Miles stand close to the casket and Miles tells Alaska that he loves her.

Chapter 36 (pp. 153–157): Miles finds himself incapable of doing anything because he feels guilty about Alaska's death. In her room, Miles is overwhelmed by the smell of her which still lingers in her belongings. Together with Chip he looks through her books and finds *The General in his Labyrinth*. He finds a passage that had been underlined by Alaska and the words 'straight and fast' scribbled in the margin. Chip and Miles think that those words might explain why she drove into the police car.

Chapter 37 (pp. 158–160): In class the teachers talk to the students and ask them how they feel. Dr Hyde reads out Alaska's question for her final essay. Miles thinks that everybody has a better excuse to grieve for Alaska than Chip and himself, since the others didn't kill her.

After reading unit 8, students can go back to the predictions made on copymaster 16 (student E) and compare them to what actually happens in the novel.

Unit 8 ➢ Copymaster 20

POSSIBLE ANSWERS

See the summary of chapters 32–37 (left).

Unit 8 ➢ Copymaster 21

NOTES

Anyone wanting more information about suicide, who has lost someone through suicide or who is suicidal can go to *www.stampoutsuicide.org.uk* (or, if they prefer a German website, *www.neuhland.net*).

1 Students may tend to criticize Chip and Miles for not having prevented Alaska's death. Here are some counter-arguments:
   - Miles and Chip wanted to prove themselves worthy of Alaska's friendship by doing what Alaska told them to.
   - Friends and relatives may help adolescents who are suicidal but will probably find it hard to prevent them from committing suicide.
   - People with suicidal tendencies need professional help.
   - It is asking too much of adolescents to show foresight in such a situation (pp. 134–135).
   - People who are determined to kill themselves will probably refuse help.

POSSIBLE ANSWERS

1 Alaska's death

p. 31, ll. 16–17: 'There are people with real problems. I've got real problems.'
p. 37, l. 28: 'I'm unpredictable.'
p. 48, ll. 21–22: 'Y'all smoke to enjoy it. I smoke to die.'
p. 56, ll. 22–23: 'I may die young,' she said. 'But at least I'll die smart.'
p. 58, ll. 17–19: 'I'm not going to be one of those people who sits around talking about what they're gonna do. I'm just going to do it.'
p. 59, l. 6: 'You never get me. That's the whole point.'
p. 86, ll. 4–7: 'It's not life or death, the labyrinth.' – 'Um, okay. So what is it?' – 'Suffering,' she said. 'Doing wrong and having wrong things happen to you.'
p. 93, l. 7–13: 'She's my hero. […] It's about depression, dumb-ass.'
p. 126, ll. 27–28: 'Pudge, what you must understand about me is that I am a deeply unhappy person.'

2–3 Individual answers.

ADDITIONAL TASKS

1 Re-writing the last scene

Now that you have read unit 8 and discussed task **2** ('Guilty or not?') of copymaster 20, re-write the last scene of unit 10 (p. 134, l. 28):

She sat down and put her head between her legs, sobbing. …

2 Speculating

Which of the following quotes could have been said by Alaska? Give reasons for your choice. (The teacher should not mention who actually said this until afterwards. That way, students may find it easier to attribute the quotes to Alaska.)

- **a** The fear of death follows from the fear of life. A man who lives fully is prepared to die at any time. (Mark Twain)
- **b** We cannot banish dangers, but we can banish fears. We must not demean life by standing in awe of death. (David Sarnoff)
- **c** The idea is to die young as late as possible. (Ashley Montagu)
- **d** Some people are so afraid to die that they never begin to live. (Henry Van Dyke)

banish verbannen

demean herabwürdigen

awe [ɔː] state of being very impressed and slightly afraid of sth.

Unit 8 – Gap Summary

TASK

Oops, something went wrong here. Can you fill in the blanks with the names of the characters in the summary below? Then put the copymaster into your reading journal with the other summaries.

The next morning ______________ wakes up all the students and asks them to come to the gym. ______________ notices that ______________ is not among the crowd. In tears, ______________ tells them that ______________ was killed in an accident the night before. Everyone is shocked and ______________ feels guilty. Incredulous, he assumes that this might be another trick ______________ is playing on them until ______________ tells him that he saw ______________ and that she had hit a police car. Walking back to his room, ______________ is aware of the fact that he will never know what ______________'s last words were.

______________ can't sleep all night and is tormented by the feeling of loss. ______________ tries to distract himself by learning things by heart. All of a sudden he leaves the room with his almanac. ______________ wonders whether he had mattered to ______________ at all and whether she had wanted to go and see ______________ that night. ______________ comes to talk to him but he doesn't want to talk to her. He has a nightmare and is all alone because ______________ hasn't returned.

Two days later ______________ returns at five a.m., freezing because he has walked 82 miles without a break. He tells ______________ that he had been fed up with ______________'s moods.

On Sunday all students attend ______________'s funeral. ______________, ______________, ______________ and ______________ go by car, avoiding the spot where ______________ died. On the way to the funeral ______________ is in tears at the idea that ______________ might have loved him back. Though he had hoped to see her again he finds the casket closed. ______________'s father tells him that she had wanted it to be that way. ______________ and ______________ stand close to the casket and ______________ tells ______________ that he loves her.

______________ finds himself incapable of doing anything because he feels guilty about ______________'s death. In her room, ______________ is overwhelmed by the smell of her which still lingers in her belongings. Together with ______________ he looks through her books and finds *The General in his Labyrinth*. He finds a passage that had been underlined by ______________ and the words 'straight and fast' scribbled in the margin. ______________ and ______________ think that those words might explain why she drove into the police car.

In class the teachers talk to the students and ask them how they feel. ______________ reads out ______________'s question for her final essay. ______________ thinks that everybody has a better excuse to grieve for ______________ than ______________ and himself, since the others didn't kill her.

© 2011 Cornelsen Verlag, Berlin. Alle Rechte vorbehalten.

Unit 8 – To Not Be Continued

TASKS

1 Alaska's death

Examine how the author prepares the reader for Alaska's death and illustrate this using quotes from the first part of the novel. Look at pages 31, 37, 48, 56, 58, 59, 86, 93 and 126.

2 Feelings of guilt

a THINK: Should Miles and Chip feel guilty about Alaska's death? Collect arguments for and against this statement.

Yes, I think they should feel guilty because …	*No, I don't think they should feel guilty because …*
______________________	______________________
______________________	______________________
______________________	______________________
______________________	______________________
______________________	______________________

b PAIR: Exchange your results with your partner and add arguments you didn't think of.

c SHARE: Discuss your statements in class. Can you come to a final conclusion? If not, explain why.

3 Putting yourself in somebody's shoes

Choose one of the following writing tasks. Give reasons for your choice.

a You are Miles

You have come back from the gym where the Eagle told the school that Alaska Young has died. You sit down and write down

– how you feel;

– what Alaska's last words might have been.

b You are 'the Eagle'

After you have told the students that Alaska Young has died in a car crash, you sit down and start writing a speech for her funeral. What are you going to say about Alaska? Write an outline.

c You are Alaska

After you have left Miles and Chip asleep in your own room, you go to their room to write a short letter to Miles. What is it you want to tell him before you leave?

4 Pre-reading unit 9

Read the words from unit 9 and speculate what Miles and Chip are going to do to find out more about Alaska's death.

phone call • police officer • research • Breathalyzer

© 2011 Cornelsen Verlag, Berlin. Alle Rechte vorbehalten.

Unit 9: Finding Out

Summary

Chapter 38 (pp. 160–162): The next day Chip tells Miles that it might have been Jake who called that night. He guesses that Alaska had wanted to go and see him and then killed herself. Miles is furious because finding out who called won't bring Alaska back. Chip sympathizes, but tells Miles that he has a plan to help them find out what happened that night. Although he doesn't really want to find out, Miles gives in because he doesn't want to lose Chip as a friend.

Chapter 39 (pp. 162–166): A few days later, Chip and Miles walk to the police station to talk to the officer who witnessed the accident. He can't tell them whether or not it was an accident. But he tells them how high her blood alcohol level was and that he saw tulips on the back seat. On their way back to school, Miles repeats that he doesn't want to find out why Alaska died. He doesn't think Chip understands him. Chip convinces him that it is important for them to stay friends, so Miles agrees to help him find out more.

Chapter 40 (pp. 166–169): The next day Miles and Chip do some research on the reasons people commit suicide. They can't draw any clear conclusions from what they find on the Internet, they only know that the phone call must have influenced Alaska's decision to kill herself. Although they don't gain any new insights, Chip insists that they carry on. Another student visits them to say that she thinks Alaska has sent her a sign, which both Chip and Miles see as a rather stupid idea.

Chapter 41 (pp. 169–173): When Chip tells Miles that he wants to call Jake to find out what happened the night Alaska died, they start arguing. Miles is angry at Chip for asking why he didn't keep Alaska from leaving that night and he goes to the Smoking Hole alone. Sitting there, he remembers Alaska and everything she taught him. He is upset because he realizes that it was her who helped him become the person he is now. He walks back to the dorm where the boys apologize to each other. Chip tells him that he has changed his mind and that he has postponed calling Jake.

Chapter 42 (pp. 173–175): Dr Hyde tells the students about Karl Marx's famous quote: 'religion is the opiate of the masses'. This makes Miles consider the possibility of an afterlife and reflect on where Alaska might be now. After class he goes to McDonald's with Takumi where both admit how much they miss Alaska.

Chapter 43 (pp. 175–182): Chip wants to get drunk to find out how drunk Alaska was when she hit the police car. For this, Chip and Miles steal Mr Starnes's Breathalyzer. Takumi is annoyed that he is not allowed to take part in this plan. The two boys stay up in their room where Chip drinks as much as he can while Miles uses the Breathalyzer to measure the alcohol in his blood. In the middle of their experiment, Mr Starnes knocks on their door. They manage to fool him, but Miles has to appear before the Jury for smoking in his room. They come to the conclusion that Alaska was definitely too drunk to drive.

Chapter 44 (pp. 182–184): Because of their investigations, Miles has neglected his studies, but he doesn't really care. Chip decides they have to call Jake as he is the only one who can possibly help them find out more. They finally let Takumi in on what happened the night Alaska left.

Unit 9 ➢ Copymaster 22

NOTES

The teacher may divide the class into two groups: group 1 works on task 1, group 2 on task 2. After the assigned tasks have been completed, the teacher may hand out the 'possible answers' from these pages for each task (as solution sheets). Then students from group 1 work in pairs with students from group 2. The student from group 1 tests the student from group 2 and vice versa.

POSSIBLE ANSWERS

1 True, false or 'tralse'?

- **a** True.
- **b** Tralse/True: He suggests talking to eye witnesses, figuring out how drunk Alaska really was and finding out where she was going and why. (He will do the latter by talking to Jake, although this is not said explicitly).
- **c** True.
- **d** False: The police officer says that Alaska was already dead when they opened the car.
- **e** Tralse/False: He saw flowers and brochures but no letter.
- **f** True.
- **g** Tralse/False: use of mind-altering substances and loss of a family member
- **h** True.
- **i** True.
- **j** False: He remembers that Alaska had a great influence on him, that she changed him and that for him she embodied the Great Perhaps.

2 A good summary

A summary is a concise account of a text's main points without details, examples, direct speech or

quotes from the original text.
Rule no. 1: no direct speech: violated in l. 1.
Rule no. 2: no comment: a summary should not contain comment or judgement: violated in ll. 5, 7 and 11.
Rule no. 3: no unimportant details: a summary should only contain the most important information: violated in ll. 9–10 and 16–17.
Rule no. 4: no speculation: a summary should only contain facts, no speculation: violated in l. 13.

Unit 9 ➢ Copymaster 23

NOTES

1 Miles's moods
This task makes students aware of the fact that Miles is permanently torn between extreme feelings of rage, helplessness, wanting to give up and desperately wanting to know why or if Alaska killed herself.
In weaker groups, or if there is not enough time, this task may given to students as preparatory homework and/or the teacher might indicate page(s) and line(s) to students to help them find the relevant passages.

POSSIBLE ANSWERS

1 Miles's moods
Chapter 38: p. 160, l. 14: listless, lethargic (pulls covers over his head while Chip enthusiastically explains his plans); p. 161, l. 2: obstinate, egocentric (refuses to cooperate; doesn't want to help Chip; only thinks about himself); p. 161, ll. 6–7 ff.: furious, cynical (shouts at Chip, calls him 'the brilliant Colonel'); p. 162, l.7: frustrated, helpless (doesn't really want to help Chip, but doesn't want to lose him as a friend)
Chapter 39: p. 165, l. 8: frustrated, helpless, sad ('Maybe we should just let her be dead', doesn't want to investigate further); p. 165, l. 30: compliant ('Fine. We'll keep looking.')
Chapter 40: p. 166, l. 1: supportive (helps Chip do research on the Internet); p. 168, l. 2: cynical ('We sure are making progress.'); p. 169, l. 14: compliant, resigned (knows that fighting with Chip is useless)
Chapter 41: p. 170, ll. 7–12: furious, rebellious (doesn't want Chip to call Jake); p. 170, l. 19 / p. 171, l. 7: rude, enraged, insolent (calls Chip 'asshole', leaves, curses him 'fuck you'); p. 171, ll. 11–14: desperate, furious, outraged, confused (screams, throws chair against wall, hates Chip, but knows at the same time that he is right; hates Alaska for having left him without any answers
Chapter 42: p. 173, l. 1: peaceable, gentle (apologizes to Chip after his return to their room); pp. 174–175: helpless, taciturn (can't really express his feelings to Takumi)
Chapter 43: pp. 175–182: helpful, supportive (helps Chip steal the breathalyser in order to find out how drunk Alaska really was)
Chapter 44: pp. 182–183: resigned ('Who gives a shit?'; 'Everything's a maybe')

2 Having a heart-to-heart
Notes (Miles): tells parents about the car crash and how no one even knows whether it was an accident; says that the possibility that she killed herself torments him and makes him (and Chip) feel guilty for failing as friends; tells about Religion class and his musings on the possibility of an afterlife
Possible questions (Miles): Do you believe in an afterlife, Mom/Dad? What happens to us when we die? I feel so guilty, what can I do? One moment I am furious, the next I am completely desperate, I don't know what to think, what can I do?
Notes (mother/father/counsellor): wants to help, takes his worries seriously, tries to suggest things he might do to relieve his grief and, at the same time advises him not to neglect his studies
Possible questions (mother/father/counsellor): Who knew her best? Do you think talking to her parents (they don't know Alaska's mother is dead) might help? How are the others coping? Why do you think they are coping differently from you? How would you feel if you found out Alaska's death was/wasn't suicide?
Possible advice (mother/father/counsellor): Try not to let yourself be overcome by grief. Decide on a time of day that you dedicate to Alaska and use it to remember her or things you did together, maybe even write down what you want to remember, maybe write her a letter with things you would have liked to tell her had you known she was going to die. Then try to dedicate the rest of your time to your studies, your friends and everything else. I'm not saying this for fear your grades might get worse, but to help protect you. Grief can be very powerful and it's important that you don't let it take over your life.

3–4 Individual answers.

ADDITIONAL TASK

1 Working with music
Choose three or four pieces of different instrumental music (no lyrics).
Suggestions: Rodriguez Fiffe, 'Mandinga'; Ruben Gonzalez, 'Como Siento Yo'; Ibrahim Ferrer, 'Buenos Hermanos'; Gerald Garcia, 'Paganini / Caprice No. 24'; Ernesto Lecuona, 'Siboney';

Edward Elgar, 'Enigma Variations – Allegro'; Sergei Prokofiev, 'Romeo and Juliet – Masks'
Give students the following listening tasks. Then present the pieces (or parts of them) to the students.
First listening:
- Which piece do you like best? Explain why.
- For each piece of music, write down a situation or scene that comes to mind.
- Exchange results with a partner.

Second listening:
- Make notes while listening: think of unit 9 and associate a scene or situation in unit 9 with each piece of music. Explain why.
- Exchange ideas with a partner.

Note: This activity can be used at any other time while working with the novel. It can also be used as a post-reading activity, then applied to the whole novel, not only to one chapter. It makes use of an entirely different approach to working with novels and appeals to learners with a distinct musical intelligence.
In groups that have not worked with music in connection to literature before, the following words might be given to the students before the activity or as a preparatory homework.

Talking about music
- I was immediately struck by the tune/rhythm.
- My favourite piece is …
- The music tells a story / helps (me) visualize a scene / reminds me of / makes me feel …
- a unique/monotonous/moving sound/rhythm
- a lovely/striking/awkward/strange arrangement
- a captivating/sad/moving tune
- a nice/interesting/lively rhythm
- to draw inspiration from …

chamber music: music for a small group of musicians
classical music
instrumental music
sacred/church music
Dur: major (key)
Moll: minor (key)

Instruments:
Blockflöte: recorder
Bratsche/Viola: viola
Cello: cello
Cembalo: harpsichord
Flügel: grand piano
Geige: violin
Gitarre: guitar
Harfe: harp
Klarinette: clarinet
Klavier: piano
Kontrabass: (double) bass
Oboe: oboe
Orgel: organ
Pauke: kettledrum
Posaune: trombone
Querflöte: flute
Saxofon: saxophone
Schlagzeug: drums/percussion
Triangel: triangle
Trompete: trumpet
Waldhorn: French horn

Unit 9 – Comprehension

TASKS

1 True, false or 'tralse'?

Read pp. 160–173. Are the following sentences true, false or 'tralse'? If they are false or 'tralse', explain why.

- **a** When Chip tells Miles that he thinks Alaska killed herself, Miles is furious.
- **b** In order to find out the truth, Chip suggests talking to eyewitnesses as well as to Jake.
- **c** The day Alaska dies, Miles and Chip walk to the police department after dinner to talk to the police officer who witnessed the scene.
- **d** When Miles asks the police officer whether he heard Alaska say anything before she died, he says he can't remember.
- **e** The police officer says that he saw white tulips in her car, brochures from colleges and a letter.
- **f** Miles and Chip do some research on the Internet to find out why people commit suicide.
- **g** They find out that Alaska only displayed two of the warning signs: use of mind-altering substances and a sudden and dramatic decline in academic performance.
- **h** When Chip tells Miles that he is going to call Jake to find out more, the two of them get into a heated argument.
- **i** Alone at the Smoking Hole, Miles thinks of Alaska and hates her for having left him with unanswered questions.
- **j** He remembers a scene earlier that year when Alaska accompanied him to the Smoking Hole and explained the Great Perhaps to him.

2 A good summary

Read pp. 173–183 and the summary below. Point out the passages which violate certain rules of summary writing.

Dr Hyde tells the students: 'Karl Marx famously called religion the "opiate of the masses".' This statement makes Miles think about the question of a possible afterlife and of where Alaska might be now. After class he goes to McDonald's with Takumi where they admit to one another how much they miss Alaska.

Clever as he is, Chip has come up with yet another ingenious plan. He wants to get drunk to find out how drunk Alaska was when she hit the police car. To be able to do so, Chip and Miles steal Mr Starnes's breathalyser, which turns out to be quite difficult. Takumi is annoyed that he is not allowed to take part in this plan. The two boys stay up in their room where Chip drinks as much as he can while Miles uses the breathalyser to measure the amount of alcohol in his blood. Miles urges Chip on, saying he can surely outdrink a girl. In the middle of their experiment Mr Starnes knocks on their door. Luckily, they manage to fool him, but Miles has to appear before the Jury for smoking in his room. In the end they come to the conclusion that Alaska was definitely too drunk to drive, which possibly helps them overcome their feelings of guilt.

Because of their investigations, Miles has neglected his studies, but he doesn't really care. Chip decides that they have to call Jake now, because he is the only one who might help them find out more. They finally let Takumi in on what happened the night Alaska left, whereupon Takumi tells them that they shouldn't have set off the fireworks.

© 2011 Cornelsen Verlag, Berlin. Alle Rechte vorbehalten.

Unit 9 – Helping Miles

TASKS

1 Miles's moods

Go through unit 9 again and take notes on Miles's feelings and changing moods. What conclusions can you draw from your findings?

2 Having a heart-to-heart

Miles urgently wants to talk to someone about his feelings. Here are three people to whom he can talk and who might be able to help him:

A The Culver Creek college counsellor: Students can go and see him/her and ask for advice in difficult situations.

B His mother: Miles could phone his mother. He tells her everything that has happened and how he is feeling. His mother tries to give him some advice.

C His father: Miles could phone his father. He tells his father everything that has happened and how he is feeling. His father tries to give him some advice.

Work with a partner and choose the character you find most suitable for this conversation. Make notes for the dialogue, including questions you would ask (as Miles or his counsellor/mother/father) and advice you might want to give (as his counsellor/mother/father).

3 Acting out dialogues

You are either Miles or the counsellor / his mother / his father. Role-play the conversation with a partner, then act it out in front of the class. Take notes on your classmates' dialogues.

4 Assessing dialogues

Which dialogue did you find most convincing and/or helpful? Explain why.

© 2011 Cornelsen Verlag, Berlin. Alle Rechte vorbehalten.

Pre-reading unit 10

Read the following statements and circle what you think might be true. Explain why you think so.

a Chip talks to Jake who | provides them with an important piece of information. / can't tell them anything new. (chapter 45)

b Miles finally apologizes to Lara for not having talked to her. / Miles meets Lara but doesn't talk to her. (chapter 46)

c Takumi / Chip | tells Miles that he has to apologize to Lara. (chapter 48)

d Miles / Chip | is tired of finding out about Alaska's death and gives up. (chapter 49)

e Finally Miles finds an important piece of evidence | in Alaska's room. / near the payphone. (chapter 50)

Unit 10: A Doodled Flower

Summary

Chapter 45 (pp. 184–188): The following day Chip finally calls Jake to find out what Alaska told him the night she died. While Chip is on the phone, Miles and Takumi argue because Takumi is tired of Miles thinking he was the only boy Alaska cared about. Chip reports what Jake told him. They know that the phone call must have played a crucial role, but Jake can't provide them with any clues to explain why Alaska left so suddenly.

Chapter 46 (pp. 188–189): The following week Miles meets Lara by chance. She looks at him angrily, but they don't talk. Miles feels awful for ignoring her, but finding out why and how Alaska died has become his life's main focus.

Chapter 47 (pp. 189–191): Takumi, Miles and Chip go to the liquor store to buy cigarettes. Once more they all notice how much they miss Alaska.

Chapter 48 (pp. 191–194): Takumi convinces Miles to talk to Lara. Miles goes to her room and apologizes for having ignored her for so long. They go for a walk and talk about Alaska. That evening Chip, Miles, Lara and Takumi go to the Smoking Hole and throw cigarettes into the water in memory of Alaska. Again they try to figure out whether Alaska's death was an accident or suicide. Since their investigations have come to a dead end, Chip decides to give up.

Chapter 49 (pp. 194–196): Miles takes up studying for his classes again. In Religion he learns that everything that comes together falls apart, which Miles thinks about a lot. Whereas Chip has given up on finding out why Alaska died, Miles still hopes to find the answer.

Chapter 50 (pp. 196–198): While calling his parents the following Sunday from the college payphone, Miles studies the notes scribbled on the wall. He discovers a flower which Alaska must have drawn while she was talking to Jake. He shows it to Chip. Both conclude that a sudden thought she had while drawing the flower must have led to her sudden departure.

Unit 10 ➢ Copymaster 24

NOTES

Students read unit 10 at home. In class, they are then given copymaster 23 and devise comprehension questions for their classmates. In weaker groups or as a variation the teacher may ask students to look back at the pre-reading questions for unit 10 and turn them into comprehension questions. Possible answers:

- **a** Why do Takumi and Miles get into a fight?
- **b** What does Chip find out when he talks to Jake?
- **c** What happens when Miles meets Lara after Religion class?
- **d** Why does Takumi think that Miles ought to talk to Lara?
- **e** Why does Chip give up?
- **f** What does Miles discover and why might this be important?

3 Everything that comes together falls apart

- **a** In case the students' shortened URL doesn't work, the teacher can mail them the original: www.bbc.co.uk/religion/religions/buddhism/subdivisions/zen_1.shtml

POSSIBLE ANSWERS

1 Devising questions

Individual answers, see variation under 'Notes'.

2 Major and minor characters

a *Miles* is the novel's protagonist; all events are told from his perspective and the novel focuses on his development as well as his thoughts and feelings.

Some students might argue that *Alaska* can also be seen as a protagonist. She is the girl Miles falls in love with and she dominates his thoughts. At the very least, she is the second most important character. If students empathize with Alaska, they might indeed argue that she is a or the protagonist. While there may be more than one protagonist, it is difficult in this novel to empathize as fully with Alaska as with Miles, since she is only seen from the outside and through his eyes. We know little about her and this is, in fact, the book's raison d'être: trying to discover Alaska's thoughts, feelings and motives – 'looking for Alaska'.

Chip is a major, versatile, round character and a catalyst for Miles's development in the novel (without Chip's perseverance in the investigation, Miles would not have been able to accept Alaska's death and find his peace of mind at the end).

Students might argue that *Takumi* is a minor character because he isn't featured as much as Miles, Chip or Alaska. Yet he is also a round, character who develops in the course of events.

Mr Starnes, Kevin, Sara and even Lara are flat, minor characters. They show few character traits and do not develop, mainly serving as foils for the other characters (Mr Starnes, for instance, stands for the law and order that Miles, Chip and Alaska are constantly violating).

b In this unit, Takumi plays a central role. He helps Miles reflect on his behaviour and his attitudes, e.g. concerning Lara. When Miles meets Lara by accident after class (p. 188), he has a bad conscience and knows that he should talk to her. He even tries seeing things from her perspective, but can't make himself talk to her. Takumi pushes Miles to finally talk to Lara by making Miles understand that it was wrong to ignore her for so long. He also helps Miles become more empathetic by recognizing the fact that others (including Takumi) also cared about Alaska (pp. 184, ll. 21–24 and 194, ll. 15–19). John Green uses Takumi as a catalyst to help his main character take another step towards maturity.

3 Everything that comes together falls apart

a *Essence of Zen Buddhism:* 'Zen' (= meditation) means trying to understand the meaning of life immediately, i.e. without recourse to books or logic. This understanding ('enlightenment') must come from within ourselves and must be experienced; it cannot be grasped intellectually.

Although it can easily be interpreted as a threat – the eventual destruction of everything that is created – the quote can also be seen as a consolation. Even if all good things must come to an end, the quote implies that negative things don't last for ever, either. Nothing is permanent, be it suffering, sadness or simple unpleasant situations. The quote could therefore be comforting to people going through difficult periods in their lives.

b On the one hand, Alaska could have found the quote comforting. She saw life as a 'labyrinth': difficult, confusing and stressful (e.g. p. 58, l. 22) and one that meant suffering (p. 86, l. 6). It might have comforted her to see her suffering as temporary and know that any difficulties in her life (e.g. guilt for forgetting the anniversary of her mother's death) wouldn't last for ever. On the other hand, a pessimistic interpretation of the quote could have made everything worse for Alaska. She could have thought it implied that her relationship with Jake or her friendships with Chip, Miles and Takumi were doomed to end at some point.

ADDITIONAL TASKS

1 Imagine you are Lara. After meeting Miles (p. 188) you describe your feelings about this encounter to your best friend. What would you say?

2 Imagine you are Takumi. You are angry with Miles for various reasons. Write a diary about Miles and why you are angry with him.

Unit 10 – Character Analysis

TASKS

1 Devising questions

a Work in groups of four. Devise a good comprehension question for each of the six chapters. Remember: a good comprehension question cannot be answered with a single word. Write your questions on slips of paper or on a sheet and hand them to the next group of students.

b Answer the six questions you receive, then pass them on to the next group. Continue until you get your own questions back.

2 Major and minor characters

a Read the following definitions.

> The **protagonist** is the principal character in a fictional text, also called the hero/heroine.
>
> A **round character** is a character in a fictional text who is complex (i.e. has several character traits) and behaves in a lifelike way. Usually he or she develops throughout the story.
>
> **Main characters** are usually round characters.
>
> A **flat character** only has a limited number of character traits and may even just represent a single quality. **Minor characters** are usually flat characters.

Work in groups and discuss:

- Who is the protagonist of the novel?
- Who is a major character and who is a minor character?

b Taking your results from **a** into account, what is Takumi's role in this unit?

3 Everything that comes together falls apart

a Use http://tinyurl.com/4bnkdub to research Zen Buddhism. In your own words, formulate its essence in a few sentences. Then read p. 195, ll. 16–22 again and comment on the quote 'Everything that comes together falls apart.' Is it a threat or a consolation to you? Explain.

b EXTRA Speculate whether the quote might have been a consolation to Alaska. Justify your answer with quotes from the text.

Pre-reading unit 11

Collect the evidence found by Miles and Chip. What do you think is the significance of the doodled flower?

© 2011 Cornelsen Verlag, Berlin. Alle Rechte vorbehalten.

Unit 11: A Memorial Prank

Summary

Chapter 51 (pp. 198–199): Miles is frustrated because it seems he will never find the reason for Alaska's death. He and Chip decide that they should plan a prank in memory of Alaska.

Chapter 52 (pp. 199–200): Chip plans the memorial prank and presents it to Miles, Takumi and Lara.

Chapter 53 (pp. 200–202): Miles calls his father because he needs his help to carry out the prank. His father agrees to fool Mr Starnes by pretending to be Dr Morse, a university professor from Florida doing research on adolescent sexuality. Mr Starnes is fooled.

Chapter 54 (pp. 202–209): They invite a professional stripper who is going to pretend to be the professor from Florida giving a speech at Culver Creek's annual Speaker Day. The whole junior class knows about the prank, but nobody tells Mr Starnes. On Speaker Day the fake Dr Morse comes, steps up on the stage, reads out the speech Chip and Miles prepared for him and then starts stripping. After the event Mr Starnes orders Miles, Chip, Lara and Takumi to never do it again, but he takes the event in good humour.

Unit 11 ➢ Copymaster 25/26

NOTES

2 Turning your text into an art gallery

1 The teacher makes a copy of copymaster 26, cuts up the quotes from unit 11 and puts them up on the classroom walls in a random order. The snippets are intended as captions for paintings or pictures.

2 Students mill around the room in groups of three and choose a snippet they like.

3 Then ten postcards with reproductions of paintings or newspaper/magazine clippings are put in small piles for students to choose from. The more abstract the pictures are, the more challenging the task is.

4 Students choose a picture to go with their caption. The pictures are then put up on the wall above the chosen snippet. One by one, each group explains how the picture fits the snippet.

5 The pictures are then put in chronological order according to the captions. When the captions are removed, students have their own illustrated unit 11.

Note: The snippets do not contain page numbers so the students concentrate more on the text. Step 5 then becomes an additional challenge.

3 Empathizing

This task may be done individually in class or as homework. Students may be reminded of what they already know about the effect of the point of view (➢ copymasters 14–15 in unit 6).

4 The making of a story

This task may be discussed in class.

POSSIBLE ANSWERS

1 Finishing sentence starters

a … he doesn't know whether the doodled flower is significant and because he fears that he'll never find out why Alaska died.

b … decides to plan a prank in memory of Alaska.

c … Chip returns to college with a detailed plan for a prank.

d … who is to pretend to be Dr Morse, a university professor from Florida and an expert in adolescent sexuality.

e … a professional stripper passing himself off as Dr Morse, a speaker at Culver Creek's annual Speaker Day.

f … the alleged Dr Morse reads out the speech Chip and Miles prepared for him before starting to strip.

g … Mr Starnes orders Miles, Chip, Lara and Takumi to never do it again, but he takes the event in good humour.

2 Turning your text into an art gallery

Individual answers. The snippets are printed in chronological order on the copymaster. **1** p. 198; **2** p. 199; **3** p. 200; **4** p. 200; **5** p. 201; **6** p. 203; **7** p. 204; **8** p. 206; **9** p. 207; **10** pp. 207–208

3 Empathizing

a Mr Starnes orders Miles, Chip, Lara and Takumi to never do anything like it again. At the same time he acknowledges the quality of the speech and how well it captured the spirit of Alaska.

b Students may mention the fact that Mr Starnes also misses Alaska and empathizes with his students. He gives them credit for doing something in memory of Alaska that would have been worthy of her, recognizing her 'voice' in the speech.

4 The making of a story

Miles is still depressed and sad because he hasn't found an answer to his questions. The search for answers has apparently come to an end. After several rather depressing chapters, this unit contains a humorous episode so the plot can take a positive turn and prepare the reader for a less serious ending. In serious works such as tragedies, this device is called 'comic relief'. It is generally used to relieve tension, but can also underline the tragedy.

Unit 11 – Art and Empathy

TASKS

1 Finishing sentence starters

Finish the sentences below to create a summary of the four chapters.

a Miles is frustrated because …

b Together with Chip he …

c After spring break …

d Miles calls his father …

e They invite …

f On Speaker Day …

g After the event …

2 Turning your text into an art gallery

In groups of three, walk round the classroom and read the snippets your teacher has put up on the walls. They are captions for paintings or pictures in an art gallery. Choose one you like. Then choose a picture to go with your snippet. Work with another group and tell each other why you chose this caption for your painting or picture.

3 Empathizing

After the prank, Mr Starnes comes to Miles and Chip's room (pp. 208–209).

a Summarize his reaction in your own words.

b Imagine you are Mr Starnes. You are sitting in the auditorium and listening to the alleged Dr Morse's speech. Lara stands up and interrupts him, then the 'speaker' starts to strip. Describe your thoughts and feelings at that moment.

Retell this scene (p. 206, l. 26 – p. 208, l. 2) from your point of view, explaining what made you react so mildly and why you didn't punish the four students.

4 The making of a story

Explain why John Green included the story of the stripper at this point in the plot.

Pre-reading unit 12

Now that the plot has taken a positive turn, how do you think it might end?

– Miles finally finds the final clue which answers all his questions.

– Takumi provides Miles and Chip with the final clue which answers all their questions.

– Chip finds the final clue which answers all their questions.

– The novel ends without anyone finding a final clue.

© 2011 Cornelsen Verlag, Berlin. Alle Rechte vorbehalten.

Unit 11 – Art Gallery Captions

✂ ---

… and as the maples around campus began to hint of resurrection and the maintenance crew began mowing the grass in the dorm circle again …

✂ ---

… the Colonel returned from spring break with two notebooks filled with the minutiae of prank planning …

✂ ---

The Barn Night crew was intact – or as close as it ever would be …

✂ ---

So I called my dad at work, and his secretary, Paul, asked me if everything was all right …

✂ ---

He was quiet for a long time, and I looked down at Alaska's last daisy …

✂ ---

As I sat through my classes that morning, I could think of nothing else.

✂ ---

He was thirtyish, tan and wide-shouldered, with a strong jaw and a dark, close-cropped goatee.

✂ ---

We applauded. My heart beat in my chest like it wanted to applaud, too.

✂ ---

You're so hot! I weesh you'd shut up and take off your clothes.

✂ ---

… revealing Maxx …, a stunningly muscular man with an eight-pack in his stomach and bulging pec muscles, and Maxx stood before us, smiling, wearing only briefs …

✂ ---

© 2011 Cornelsen Verlag, Berlin. Alle Rechte vorbehalten.

Unit 12: Out of the Labyrinth

Summary

Chapter 55 (pp. 209–210): A week after the prank, Takumi provides Chip and Miles with the final clue about Alaska's death. He tells them that the day she left campus was January 10, the anniversary of her mother's death. They deduce that the flower she doodled on the wall while talking to Jake reminded her of the anniversary and assume she had a bad conscience for forgetting it.

Chapter 56 (pp. 210–213): Though they still don't know whether Alaska's death was suicide or an accident, they finally give up on wanting to find out. Miles and Chip decide to drive through the spot on the highway where the accident happened.

Chapter 57 (p. 213): Miles, Chip, Lara and Takumi study laboriously for their finals and Miles misses Alaska because Chip is not as good a Maths teacher as she was.

Chapter 58 (pp. 213–215): In Religion, Dr Hyde gives the students the task for their annual final paper. He asks them to discuss Alaska's central question, how to get out of 'this labyrinth of suffering'.

Chapter 59 (pp. 215–219): One day before his parents come to pick him up, Miles finds a letter from Takumi, telling him and Chip that he was mad at them because they did not include him in their investigations about Alaska's death. He reveals that he met Alaska just before she got into her car the night she died. She had been looking for flowers to put on her mother's grave. Having read Takumi's letter, Miles understands that one crucial aspect of coping with life is forgiveness. With this insight, he is able to write his final essay in one go. He is at peace with himself knowing that he will never know whether her death was an accident or suicide, but he understands that he doesn't have to feel guilty about it any longer.

Unit 12 ➢ Copymaster 27

POSSIBLE ANSWERS

1 A; **2** D; **3** A and D; **4** A and B; **5** C; **6** B and C; **7** C; **8** B and C

Unit 12 ➢ Copymaster 28

NOTES

1 The labyrinth of suffering
The teacher reminds students of ➢ copymaster 11. If students did not receive it in unit 4, the teacher can hand it out now.

POSSIBLE ANSWERS

1 The labyrinth of suffering
Individual answers.

2 Twenty years later

a Miles and Chip meet at the 'Megacities in Close-Up Conference' in New York.
Miles is a free-lance journalist, he writes articles for magazines like *The Nation* or *The Scientific American* or *The New Yorker*. His love for books and famous people's last words influenced his decision to study Journalism and History. He is at the conference to write an article about lectures given by two famous researchers. Married with two children and living in Boston, Miles lives the settled life of an East Coast intellectual. He is quite happy with his life and with what he has achieved.
The year at Culver Creek had a lasting effect on Miles. Chip, Alaska and Takumi helped him gain self-confidence and made him understand how important friends are and what friendship means. Alaska still haunts him: he was mostly attracted to girls who reminded him of her.
Chip is a geographer. He works for The Unites States Geographical Survey, a scientific organization that compiles unbiased information about environmental issues. He studied Geography and spent a lot of time abroad as a researcher. He is not married but is very successful in his job and a well-known expert in the gentrification in megacities. He is quite happy, although he would like to settle down and have a family instead of travelling around so much.
Chip has spent most of his life alone. He thinks about Miles and the others now and then.

b *Questions they might ask each other:* How are you? What are you doing here? Do you have a family? Are you still in touch with anybody from Culver Creek?
What they might like to tell each other: that they were and still are grateful for each other's friendship at Culver Creek.

3 Dealing with a review

a *Positive aspects:* exciting; full of suspense, philosophical ideas, tough everyday issues and surprising plot twists; forces the reader to re-think their first impressions of the characters; makes the reader truly think about life

Negative aspects: plot takes a long time to reach its climax

b Individual answers.

4 Parts of a sum

a Everybody is greater than the sum of his/her parts. There are people who create something: they write books, or music, there are artists who create paintings or sculptures, architects who design houses, scientists who make inventions which save lives. The books, the music, the pieces of art, the architecture, the inventions often have a lasting, maybe even life-saving effect on others. So a part of these people (who may have died) live on in their creations.

If students find it difficult to develop their own ideas, the teacher might suggest the names of famous people who created something that had a lasting effect (e.g. Marc Zuckerberg).

Students might argue that they aren't famous and that they haven't created anything with a lasting effect yet. Then the teacher might ask them to think about all their friends and family and of people who have or had a lasting effect on them and why. If students consider this question to be too personal, they may do it in writing.

ADDITIONAL TASKS

1 Energy is never created and never destroyed

Ask your Physics teacher to explain the law of the conservation of energy to you. If possible, ask him or her to give you some examples. Then reread p. 219, ll. 4–9 and explain them with the help of your knowledge of physics.

Unit 12 – Let's Get It Right

TASK

Choose the correct answer or answers.

1 A week and a half after the prank, Takumi points out to Miles that

- ☐ **A** Alaska told them on Barn Night that her mother died the day after taking her to the zoo on January 9.
- ☐ **B** for Alaska, the best and the worst day were the same.
- ☐ **C** Alaska wanted to die on the anniversary of her mother's death.
- ☐ **D** Alaska died on the anniversary of her mother's death.

2 Talking things over, Takumi, Miles and Chip

- ☐ **A** decide that it must have been suicide.
- ☐ **B** decide that it was an accident.
- ☐ **C** realize that this doesn't help them decide whether it was suicide or an accident.
- ☐ **D** come up with two plausible scenarios.

3 Chip and Miles borrow Takumi's car

- ☐ **A** in order to drive past the scene of the accident.
- ☐ **B** in order to go to Vine Station.
- ☐ **C** in order to go to McDonald's.
- ☐ **D** in order to do what Alaska did.

4 The final exams are approaching and

- ☐ **A** Miles misses Alaska.
- ☐ **B** Miles, Lara, Takumi and Chip study hard together.
- ☐ **C** all four of them read *Things Fall Apart* and *A Farewell to Arms*.
- ☐ **D** Takumi fails precalc.

5 Dr Hyde

- ☐ **A** asks his students to answer Alaska's essay question referring to Taoism, Judaism and Hinduism.
- ☐ **B** gives the students more time to write their final papers.
- ☐ **C** gives the students Alaska's essay question.
- ☐ **D** cancels final exams in memory of Alaska.

6 Takumi writes a letter to Miles and Chip in which he tells them that

- ☐ **A** Alaska talked about them the night she left.
- ☐ **B** being left out of their plans hurt him.
- ☐ **C** he met Alaska just before she left.
- ☐ **D** he knows that it was suicide.

7 After reading the letter, Miles

- ☐ **A** tries to find Chip.
- ☐ **B** is more confused than ever.
- ☐ **C** realizes something.
- ☐ **D** is mad at Takumi.

8 Having read Takumi's letter, Miles writes his final essay in which he

- ☐ **A** discusses the law of the conservation of energy.
- ☐ **B** finally understands that the way out of the labyrinth is forgiveness.
- ☐ **C** finds a way out of the labyrinth for himself.
- ☐ **D** discovers how Alaska died.

© 2011 Cornelsen Verlag, Berlin. Alle Rechte vorbehalten.

Unit 12 – Looking Back at the Novel

TASK

1 The labyrinth of suffering

'How will you – you personally – ever get out of this labyrinth of suffering?' (p. 214, ll. 4–7). Write a short comment of about 300 words stating your thoughts on Alaska's question. Bear in mind what you have learned about the composition of texts.

2 Twenty years later

a Read the following scenario and questions and take notes for your answer. Then write a short paragraph about either Miles or Chip.

Miles and Chip, now both about forty years old, meet at a conference for the first time since their graduation from Culver Creek Preparatory School. Consider:
– what kind of conference it might be;
– the jobs they have;
– what their lives look like now;
– whether they are married and/or have children;
– whether they are happy and/or successful in their jobs;
– how they view their time at Culver Creek from their perspective as adults.

Did Alaska's death have a lasting effect on them? Give reasons for your answer.

b Then work with a partner who chose the other character and talk to each other. Your text from **a** may help you. Which questions would you like to ask your partner? Is there something either Miles or Chip would like to tell the other which he couldn't say when he was young?

3 Dealing with a review

a Read the following excerpt from a review of *Looking for Alaska*. In your own words, explain what the reviewer likes and dislikes about the novel.

> John Green's slow-to-the-punch yet devastatingly arresting debut novel is a prime example of what happens when a writer intertwines seemingly ordinary characters with a storyline that is ripe with philosophical musings, hard-hitting life issues, and a shocking plot twist that will compel readers to re-examine their previous conceptions about the book and its characters, and give them ample space to think – *really* think – about what it means to be alive and present in the world.

From: Alexis Burling on www.teenreads.com/reviews/0525475060.asp

slow-to-the-punch taking a long time to come to the climax
devastatingly *(adv, here)* extremely
intertwine sich verflechten, verschlingen
musing *(n, usu pl)* Grübeln
ample enough or more than enough

b Do you agree with the reviewer? Explain why or why not.

4 Parts of a sum

In his final essay, Miles writes that 'we are greater than the sum of our parts' (p. 218, ll. 31–32). What is it that makes you greater than the sum of your parts? What would your friends say if they were asked this question about you?

© 2011 Cornelsen Verlag, Berlin. Alle Rechte vorbehalten.

Post-reading Activities

1 Reading poster

Note: A reading poster offers students the possibility of visualizing the content and their interpretation of a novel read in class. Students choose which elements of the plot they want to portray in which way and in which order. They can focus on the characters, problems or situations they found particularly interesting. The poster may be drawn, painted or presented as a zigzag book *(Leporello)*, a photo story or a collage of pictures cut out of magazines and newspapers. Students may be given suggestions, but are free to choose the form of presentation they like best. The poster may only mirror the plot, but can also include a personal appreciation of the novel. The posters may be produced by individual students or in groups.

Aim: presenting the plot; recapitulating the novel; reacting to the novel; visualizing problems and/or relationships; focussing on major events and key scenes including quotes and/or key words

Task: Portray your interpretation of *Looking for Alaska* on a reading poster. You may use watercolours, crayons and pictures from magazines and the Internet. You may include relevant quotes, but your poster should mainly represent visual elements. If you wish, you can present your poster to the class.

2 Quote hunt

Aim: highlighting the most important parts of the novel; recalling details, especially before written tests

Preparation: The teacher collects 10–15 important sentences from the novel and presents them in chronological order (otherwise the activity might prove too difficult).

Task: Read the quotes and explain who said this in which context and why.

3 Blurbs

Aim: understanding the function of blurbs (i.e. arousing curiosity by stating the most important facts very briefly)

Task: Write a blurb for *Looking for Alaska*. You may include a quote from the text that underlines your intention.

4 Book on a postcard

Aim: briefly stating your own opinion

Task: In approximately 50 words (so that it would fit onto a postcard), review the book you have just read.

Note: This is not a summary but your opinion.

5 Write and respond

Aim: putting yourself in somebody's shoes; creative writing

Task: Choose a character from *Looking for Alaska* that you liked, disliked or found difficult to understand. Write a letter to him or her, asking questions about their behaviour or particular incidents. Give your letter to a classmate and ask him or her to answer your letter from the character's point of view.

6 Acrostic

Aim: describing a character; activating vocabulary

Preparation: Write the names of the major characters (Miles, Chip, Alaska, Takumi) vertically on the board.

Task: For each character on the board, write a characterization by using the individual letters of each name as the first letter of a descriptive adjective.

Example:

Conscious of his and others' social status
Honest
Intelligent
Poor

7 Poems

a Diamond poem

Aim: expressing ideas creatively

Task: Use the pattern below. Start with the two nouns at either end: they must be clear opposites (e.g. 'before' and 'after', or opposite ideas, characters, places in the novel). Then fill in adjectives and participles which are related to the nouns on their side of the diamond. With the third participle, students start expressing the opposite before moving towards the other end of the diamond. The resulting poem expresses development between two opposing concepts from the novel.

noun

adjective   adjective   adjective

participle   participle   participle   participle

adjective   adjective   adjective

noun

Example:

Florida

temperate boring minor

stagnating studying learning changing

boiling exciting serious

Alabama

b Biography poem

Aim: describing a character; activating vocabulary

Task: Write a poem about a character in the novel using the following example:

1	(name)	*'The Eagle'*
2	(three descriptive adjectives)	*Strict, demanding, kind*
3	Who loves …	Who loves *his school*
4	Who wants …	Who wants *his students to succeed*
5	Always …, never …	Always *vigilant*, never *tiring*
6	(name)	'The Eagle'

You may also devise different, more challenging patterns for the biography poem.

c Haiku

Aim: limiting yourself, channelling your creativity

Description: Haikus consist of three lines and between twelve and seventeen syllables in total. In a traditional Japanese haiku, the first line contains five syllables, the second contains seven (up to nine in a non-traditional haiku), and the third five syllables. Haikus present an object in nature and an emotion or a surprising observation that accompanies the perception of that object. Traditionally, a haiku also includes a word or phrase that conveys the season of the poem.

Task: Write a haiku that either expresses how you feel about the novel or one that mirrors a situation or a character's feeling in a certain situation.

Example: An old barn at night
Intimate rage glowing in faces
Best and worst are told

8 Book cover

Aim: visually expressing contents

Task: You are a graphic designer and are to design a new cover for *Looking for Alaska*. It should express the spirit of the book and appeal to potential readers. Create an example and present it to your class, explaining your choice.

9 Pick a pocket

Aim: guessing characteristics

Preparation: Bring some items that you usually carry (or might carry) in your (hand)bag/pocket (e.g. a pair of sunglasses, a coin from your last summer holiday, a lipstick, a tiny address book, two hazelnuts).

Task: Look at the objects. What do they reveal about their owner and his or her character? Work with a partner. Choose a character from *Looking for Alaska* and speculate what they might have carried around with them.

10 Rewrite it

Aim: recognizing the essence of a novel

Task: Rewrite (the essence of) *Looking for Alaska* in another genre, e.g. as a fairy tale, a fable, a poem (see under **7**) or a news report.

11 Guessing game

Aim: stimulating the imagination

Preparation: Bring along a large number of picture postcards, pictures from magazines, etc. In pairs, students choose a postcard they like. Then give them the task (this is important!).

Task: Work with a partner and choose a picture. Think of a character, an abstract idea, a place, a problem you encountered while reading the novel. The more abstract your idea is the better. Then relate it to the picture you chose. The rest of the class / another pair asks questions to find out what each pair saw in the postcard. The pair that is being questioned may only answer with *yes* or *no*.

Example: Pair A chooses a picture of an angry old man. They think of the scene in which Dr Hyde throws Miles out of his class. Pair B / The rest of the class asks yes/no questions to find out what Pair A thought of when looking at the picture.

Ideas for Projects ➢ Copymaster 29

1 Looking for the author

The teacher makes sure that some students do task **a** and others task **b**. He or she can tell them the following to help them with their decision: Choose task **a** to learn what John Green read while growing up ('Interview 2') and what he thinks is the future of the book ('Interview 5'). Choose task **b** if you want to find out why *Looking for Alaska* was controversial.

In case the students' shortened URLs don't work, the teacher can mail them the original ones.

For **a**: www2.scholastic.com/browse/video.jsp?pID=1640183585&bcpid=1640183585&bclid=21506639001&bctid=21392220001;

for **b**: www.youtube.com/user/vlogbrothers#p/search/5/fHMPtYvZ8tM.

b As this video is rather long (four minutes), the teacher should stop it as often as necessary and play it at least twice.

For a task analysing the scenes mentioned by Green (p. 128, l. 22 – p. 131, l. 24 and p. 132, l. 4 – p. 134, l. 13) that were criticized by some parents, see unit 7, additional task **2** (p. 41).

Note: 'Vlogbrothers' is a project that John Green started with his brother Hank (addressed in this video), initially only for a year. They wanted to test this new medium and restricted their communication to 'vlogging' for an entire year. Because of its success, they continued their project afterwards and are still using it on a daily basis.

2 Suicide in religion

The teacher divides the class into six groups and has them work in a jigsaw mode (see 'Note' below). The students in each group are labelled from A–E. They do research on their topic (at home or at school) and compile their results, e.g. on a poster.

Note: *Jigsaw puzzle:* Students form new groups. Each one should include a member of each initial group (all As/Bs etc. form a new group). One group's results are discussed. The student from this particular group (the 'group expert') explains their results to the other students and answers questions. Upon a signal from the teacher, the next group's results are examined, presented by the new group expert. The activity is over when all results have been presented. As a follow-up, the most important results are collected in class.

Variation: Students with an interest in art may form a seventh group and research depictions of suicide in religious art (e.g. Giotto's 'Despair' or 'Desperation', one of the seven vices).

3 Works cited or alluded to in *Looking for Alaska*

Students work in groups, do research and present their findings in a gallery walk.

Note: *Gallery walk:* Groups move from station to station, taking three to five minutes at each station to brainstorm and collect different ideas, note them down and reflect on other groups' ideas, noting down their reactions to them. Back at the station they started from, each group organizes the information collected, discusses it and presents it to the class. Alternatively, the results are commented on in a class discussion.

Variation: Advanced students may read one of the books or poems mentioned below and present it to the class.

p. 9: François Rabelais, last words

p. 14: Robert Frost, poem 'Stopping by Woods on a Snowy Evening'

p. 15: Henrik Ibsen, last words

p. 22: Gabriel García Márquez, *The General in His Labyrinth*

p. 28: Bob Woodward, Carl Bernstein, *The Final Days* (about Richard Nixon and Watergate; for advanced students interested in recent American history)

p. 63: Herman Melville, *Moby Dick*

p. 78: Charlotte Brontë, *Jane Eyre*

p. 93, ll. 15–16: Shakespeare, *Richard III*

p. 85: Kurt Vonnegut, *Cat's Cradle*

p. 89: W.H. Auden, poem 'As I Walked Out One Evening'

p. 92: Edna St Vincent Millay, poem 'Not So Far as the Forest'

p. 199: William Faulkner, *The Sound and the Fury*

p. 213: Chinua Achebe, *Things fall Apart*

p. 213: Ernest Hemingway, *A Farewell to Arms*

4 More last words

a William Somerset Maugham (1874–1965, English novelist and short story writer); **b** Oscar Wilde (1854–1900, Irish poet and writer); **c** Heinrich Heine (1797–1856, German poet and critic); **d** Karl Marx (1818–1883, German political theorist, communist revolutionary and philosopher); **e** Leonardo da Vinci (1452–1519, Italian allround genius); **f** Jean-Baptiste Camille Corot (1796–1875, French painter)

Ideas for Projects – Thinking Things Out

TASKS

1 Looking for the author

a Work in pairs and go to http://tinyurl.com/3xuoa8l. One of you watches 'Interview 2', the other 'Interview 5'. Take notes on what John Green says. Exchange your notes, then present your results to those who did task **b**.

b 1 Pre-viewing: Look up the word 'nerd' in a monolingual dictionary. What could a 'nerdfighter' be? With your partner, go to http://tinyurl.com/64vmvv3. Watch Green's vlog and take notes.

2 While viewing:

- a Describe the measures taken by Depew High School after their decision to teach *Looking for Alaska* in class.
- b Explain Green's argument for why the sexually explicit passage is not pornographic.
- c Describe Green's reason for including the sexually explicit passage in the novel. What did he want to achieve by contrasting it to another scene?
- d Explain the two expressions 'physical intimacy' and 'emotional closeness'.
- e Sum up Green's argument against those who think 'teenagers are unable to read critically'.
- f Point out what Green wishes to achieve with this vlog entry.

2 Suicide in religion

Choose a religion: Buddhism, Christianity: Protestantism, Christianity: Catholicism, Hinduism, Islam, Judaism. Then work in groups and research how suicide is regarded by each religion. Present your findings, e.g. on a poster. Which religious approach would have appealed to Alaska? Which approach appeals to you?

3 Works cited or alluded to in *Looking for Alaska*

Work in pairs or groups and research the authors/poets and their books, plays, poems or last words mentioned in *Looking for Alaska*. Your teacher will give you a list. Make a poster about the author/poet and his or her text. Include your thoughts on why this particular text might have been mentioned.

4 More last words

Read the following quotes of famous people's last words and choose the one you like best. Explain why you like it. What kind of person could have said those words? Your teacher will tell you whose last words they were. Then compare this with your speculations on the person. Do research if necessary.

a 'Dying is a very dull, dreary affair. And my advice to you is to have nothing whatever to do with it.'

b 'Either that wallpaper goes or I do.'

c 'God will pardon me. It's his profession.'

d 'Go on, get out. Last words are for fools who haven't said enough.'

e 'I have offended God and mankind because my work did not reach the quality it should have.'

f 'I hope with all my heart there will be painting in heaven.'

© 2011 Cornelsen Verlag, Berlin. Alle Rechte vorbehalten.

Written Tests

Suggestions for testing students' reading and writing skills in connection with the novel

Written Test 1 (Dealing with an extract from the novel) ➢ Copymaster 30

NOTE

2 Analysis

This task is for advanced students of a *Leistungskurs*. In grade 10 or a *Grundkurs*, the teacher may leave it out.

3 Comment/Composition

b The text type here may resemble an interior monologue. If the teacher wants to, he or she can introduce the term beforehand, e.g. using the definition below.

Interior monologue: a particular kind of scenic presentation in which the author depicts the thoughts and feelings passing through a character's mind. Often an interior monologue does not follow a chronological order, because when people think, their thoughts jump from one subject to another. The more common way of portraying thought is through 'reported thought', in which the thoughts are presented as reported speech, introduced by reporting verbs like 'think'.

POSSIBLE ANSWERS

1 Comprehension

- Miles imagines the scene of how eight-year-old Alaska found her mother lying on the ground, convulsing.
- Imagining the scene helps him to understand Alaska's thoughts and feelings – and her impulsive nature.
- Miles thinks about what Alaska has told them and reflects on the meaning of the events for Alaska and her life.
- Alaska's mother died because Alaska didn't call an ambulance.
- He understands that this incident had a formative influence.
- From then on, she was constantly afraid of being paralyzed, unable to make decisions in time.
- He understands that this is the labyrinth she can't escape and which causes her suffering.
- Yet, he doesn't talk to her about his thoughts and the evening continues as though nothing out of the ordinary had happened.

2 Analysis

Repetition/Anaphora: ll. 1–2: When she ..., I knew what she meant / when she ..., I knew whom she meant; ll. 2–3: the everything / the everyone; ll. 11, 15, 15–16: We are all going; l. 17: not / not

Allusion: l. 15, 'labyrinth of suffering': an allusion to Simón Bolívar's last words as quoted by Alaska from García Márquez' *The General in His Labyrinth*; l. 18, 'night fell fast': an allusion to Edna St Vincent Millay's poem which Alaska quoted to Miles ('Night falls fast. Today is in the past.', ➢ copymaster 13).

Interpretation: The repetitions underline the respective statement, making it stronger and more forceful (e.g. we really *are* all going). The anaphora in ll. 1–2 serves to structure Miles's thoughts, he is seeking to structure what before seemed unclear and chaotic to him: Alaska's behaviour. The allusion to Millay's poem foreshadows Alaska's death, as does Miles's interpretation of Bolívar's labyrinth of suffering.

3 Comment/Composition

a *Comment:*

- This quote summarizes Miles's realization; it is the climax of the extract.
- Miles finally understands that death is inevitable and that nobody can save us from it.
- He considers this – that we all must die – to be the labyrinth of suffering from which everyone has to find their own exit. Alternatively, 'Find your way out of that maze' can be understood as a further reinforcement of the previous statement, as a sort of ironic request: try to find your way out of that maze (i.e. see whether you are immortal) – you will fail.

Would you agree: Individual answers.

b 'There, I finally did it, I said it. Now they all know. What a good idea to play the game; it's so good to finally have told someone. But I've also revealed an important part of me. Will they still like me? Will they think I'm weak? Or can it really help them to understand my motives better? Maybe I shouldn't have told them. It doesn't help anyone. It doesn't help me find a way out of the labyrinth and it doesn't help them. Nothing I say or do can ever make her alive again. I failed completely. Can they even begin to understand what that means? But Pudge and the Colonel are my friends, they should know. Maybe they can help me get out of this labyrinth of suffering, after all. If there is a way out ...'

Written Test 2 (Dealing with an extract from another novel) ➢ Copymaster 31

NOTE

3 Comment

More advanced students can be given the following task:

'I am Outcast.' (l. 24). First, discuss what makes someone an outsider. Then, based on your knowledge of the novel *Looking for Alaska*, discuss which of the characters could have said this about him- or herself.

Possible answer:

Miles could have said this about himself at the beginning of the novel: he must have felt like an outsider at his old school. At Culver Creek he soon finds new friends who like him the way he is and make him feel good about himself; he gains self-confidence.

Alaska might have said this about herself, fearing to become an outcast after she told the Eagle about Paul and Marya. But even before that, she had character traits that might make it difficult for her to be popular, especially with other girls: she has strong views about how girls should behave; she doesn't show typical traits of female teenagers (she drinks and smokes a lot, she is good at mathematics; she talks about sex openly and without inhibition); she is moody and calculating and sometimes treats her friends unfairly. Her personal circumstances also seem to further the view of Alaska as an outsider: she doesn't have a proper home where she can go during her holidays and seems to have to fend for herself; she seems caught in her labyrinth of suffering.

POSSIBLE ANSWERS

1 Comprehension

It is Melinda's first school day at high school. She enters the bus, but doesn't know where to sit. When other students enter the bus, many of whom she knows from middle school, nobody wants to sit next to her. During the bus ride, someone throws a wrapper at her. After the bus has dropped the students off at school, they form different cliques. The narrator doesn't belong to any of the groups; she even spent most of her summer holidays on her own at home. Melinda feels outcast because no one talks to her, she doesn't belong to any group, and the only attention she gets is negative attention.

(110 words)

2 Analysis

Point of view: first-person narrator; limited point of view: reader sees everything through the eyes of the narrator, i.e. the protagonist

Effect on the reader:

- makes the reader empathize with Melinda, pity her, show compassion, develop a dislike for the other students who treat her unkindly;
- makes the reader want to find out why Melinda is or became an outcast, want to know what happened, want to read on;
- creates suspense / builds tension.

3 Comment/Composition

Assess Melinda and Miles's situation: Melinda seems to be an outcast at her school. The others know her but ignore her completely for something that must have happened in the past. Her situation seems rather hopeless and Melinda seems to be aware of that; as she expected to be an outcast, she seems to accept her fate.

Miles wants to go to a new school to find new friends and to look for 'a Great Perhaps', new opportunities. He seems to be willing to make new friends and is open to new people, situations and experiences.

Examine how Miles's situation changes at Culver Creek: While Melinda seems to have given up and accepted her fate, Miles does something to change it. For Miles, this undertaking proves successful: He joins a peer group, dares flout the rules of the college, plays pranks and has the feeling that he found what he was looking for at Culver Creek. When Chip and Alaska accept him the way he is, he gains self-confidence.

Written Test 1

NAME: **CLASS:** **WRITTEN TEST NO:** **DATE:**

Extract from *Looking for Alaska* by John Green

two days before

[…] It was the central moment of Alaska's life. When she cried and told me that she fucked everything up, I knew what she meant now. And when she said she failed everyone, I knew whom she meant. It was the everything and the everyone of her life, and so I could not help but imagine it: I imagined a scrawny eight-year-old with dirty fingers, looking down at her mother convulsing. So she sat down with her dead-or-maybe-not mother, who I imagine was not breathing by then but wasn't yet cold either. And in the time between dying and death, a little Alaska sat with her mother in silence. And then through the silence and my drunkenness, I caught a glimpse of her as she might have been. She must have come to feel so powerless, I thought, that the one thing she might have done – pick up the phone and call an ambulance – never even occurred to her. There comes a time when we realize that our parents cannot save themselves or save us, that everyone who wades through time eventually gets dragged out to sea by the undertow – that, in short, we are all going. So she became impulsive, scared by her inaction into perpetual action. When the Eagle confronted her with expulsion, maybe she blurted out Marya's name because it was the first that came to mind, because in that moment she didn't want to get expelled and couldn't think past that moment. She was scared, sure. But more importantly, maybe she'd been scared of being paralyzed by fear again. 'We are all going,' McKinley said to his wife, and we sure are. There's your labyrinth of suffering. We are all going. Find your way out of that maze.

None of which I said out loud to her. Not then and not ever. We never said another word about it. Instead, it became just another worst day, albeit the worst of the bunch, and as night fell fast, we continued on, drinking and joking.

From: John Green, *Looking for Alaska*, 2010 (first published in 2005)

3 *scrawny:* very thin **4** *convulse:* cause a sudden shaking movement in sb.'s body **10** *undertow (n):* Sog **11** *perpetual:* continuing for a long period of time without interruption **12** *blurt sth. out:* say sth. suddenly and without thinking carefully enough **14** *paralyzed*: unable to feel or move **18** albeit: although

© 2011 Cornelsen Verlag, Berlin. Alle Rechte vorbehalten.

TASKS

1 Comprehension

In no more than 80–100 words, summarize the extract in your own words.

2 Analysis

Analyse the stylistic devices used in the extract and explain their effect on the reader.

3 Comment/Composition

Answer either **a** or **b**.

a Comment on the quote 'There's your labyrinth of suffering. We are all going. Find your way out of that maze.' (ll. 15–16) in the context of the extract above.
Would you agree that we live in a 'labyrinth of suffering'? Why or why not?

b After Alaska has told her friends about her best and her worst day, everybody remains quiet, thinking about what she has told them. Using a first-person point of view, write down Alaska's thoughts and feelings at that moment.

Written Test 2

NAME: **CLASS:** **WRITTEN TEST NO:** **DATE:**

Extract from *Speak* by Laurie Halse Anderson

WELCOME TO MERRYWEATHER HIGH

It is my first morning of high school. I have seven new notebooks, a skirt I hate, and a stomachache.

The school bus wheezes to my corner. The door opens and I step up. I am the first pickup of the day. The driver pulls away from the curb while I stand in the aisle. Where to sit? I've never been a backseat wastecase. If I sit in the middle, a stranger could sit next to me. If I sit in the front, it will make me look like a little kid, but I figure it's the best chance I have to make eye contact with one of my friends, if any of them have decided to talk to me yet.

The bus picks up students in groups of four or five. As they walk down the aisle, people who were my middle-school lab partners or gym buddies glare at me. I close my eyes. This is what I've been dreading. As we leave the last stop, I am the only person sitting alone.

The driver downshifts to drag us over the hills. The engine clanks, which makes the guys in the back holler something obscene. Someone is wearing too much cologne. I try to open my window, but the little latches won't move. A guy behind me unwraps his breakfast and shoots the wrapper at the back of my head. It bounces into my lap – a Ho-Ho.

We pass janitors painting over the sign in front of the high school. The school board has decided that 'Merryweather High – Home of the Trojans' didn't send a strong abstinence message, so they have transformed us into the Blue Devils. Better the Devil you know than the Trojan you don't, I guess. School colors will stay purple and gray. The board didn't want to spring for new uniforms.

Older students are allowed to roam until the bell, but ninth-graders are herded into the auditorium. We fall into clans: Jocks, Country Clubbers, Idiot Savants, Cheerleaders, Human Waste, Eurotrash, Future Fascists of America, Big Hair Chix, the Marthas, Suffering Artists, Thespians, Goths, Shredders. I am clanless. I wasted the last weeks of August watching bad cartoons. I didn't go to the mall, the lake, or the pool, or answer the phone. I have entered high school with the wrong hair, the wrong clothes, the wrong attitude. And I don't have anyone to sit with.

I am Outcast.

There is no point looking for my ex-friends. Our clan, the Plain Janes, has splintered and the pieces are being absorbed by rival factions. Nicole lounges with the Jocks, comparing scars from summer league sports. Ivy floats between the Suffering Artists on one side of the aisle and the Thespians on the other. She has enough personality to travel with two packs. Jessica has moved to Nevada. No real loss. She was mostly Ivy's friend, anyway.

From: Laurie Halse Anderson, *Speak*, New York: Farrar, Straus and Giroux, 1999

2 *wheeze*: breathe noisily and with difficulty **3** *curb:* Bordstein **3** *aisle:* space between rows of seats **3** *wastecase (sl):* loser **8** *glare at sb./sth.*: (wütend) anstarren **8** *dread* (v): (be)fürchten **10** *downshift* (AE): change to a lower gear **10** *holler* (AE): shout **11** *latch:* Riegel **13** *Ho-Ho:* type of chocolate cake **14** *janitor* (AE): caretaker **15** *Trojan:* brand name of most popular US condoms **15** *abstinence:* the practice of not having sex before marriage **16** *better the devil you know:* allusion to the proverb which ends 'than the devil you don't' **17** *spring for:* pay for **24** *outcast:* person rejected by others **25** *Plain Jane*: average girl **25** *splinter* (v): break up into pieces **26** *lounge with sb.* (here): hang around with sb.

Tasks

1 Comprehension

Read the beginning of the novel *Speak* above ('I' = Melinda). In no more than 150 words, summarize the extract in your own words.

2 Analysis

Analyse the point of view and its effect on the reader.

3 Comment/Composition

Assess Melinda and Miles's situation at the beginning of term. Examine how Miles's situation changes at Culver Creek.

© 2011 Cornelsen Verlag, Berlin. Alle Rechte vorbehalten.